ENDORSEMENTS FOR
MOONLIGHT ON THE GANGA

Jean Houston, Ph.D., author of *Jump Time* and *A Passion for the Possible*:

"This work flows with the wisdom and depth of the most sacred of all rivers."

Lynn Andrews, best-selling author of the Medicine Woman series and *Love and Power*:

"*Moonlight on the Ganga* brings the sacred flow of the Ganga into the illuminating current of spiritual power within each of us."

Reverend Dr. Lauren Artress, author of *Walking A Sacred Path*, and creator of *The Labyrinth Project*:

"*Moonlight on the Ganga* is lush in imagery, bold in articulating experience and allows the reader to reflect on the spiritual essence of his or her own life."

Geoffrey Fox, author of *Hispanic Nation: Culture, Politics and the Constructing of Identity*, and *Welcome to My Contri*:

"Like a Sufi poem in prose, *Moonlight on the Ganga* illuminates the murky recesses of the soul and surprises us by finding the extraordinary in the most mundane of events."

Sheila Bender, author of *Writing Personal Essays: How to Shape Your Life Experience for the Page* and *A Year in the Life: Journaling for Self-Discovery*:

"In India, when the rich traditions of knowledge were first placed into written form, Krulikowski tells us, it was on palm leaves and tree bark displayed together and hung in cords. So, too, Ms. Krulikowski's lyric, evocative essays about her life-changing trip to Rishikesh on the Ganges hang together, each one with sparkling gems of insight that enter the reader as easily as water."

Sabrina Fox, author of *Loved By Angels* and *Who Can Help Me Sleep*:

"Claire's willingness to let us share her time on the Ganga, without leaving us out of the most intimate of journeys—self discovery—is a great honor and an inspiration. You can almost feel the crisp touch of the Ganga's water on your feet as Claire opens up her soul for us to share in her exquisite journey."

Jo Dunning, teacher of The Expanded Heartworks:

"This book is a delightful story of travel, insight, and personal expansion. It's words flow smoothly, like the Ganga, creating a feeling of peaceful calm as each page unfolds its beauty and wisdom."

Suzane Piela, author of *You Are So Beautiful Without Your Hair*:

"At a time when our society is searching for deeper meaning, this book is certain to provide much food for thought."

MOONLIGHT
ON THE GANGA

MOONLIGHT ON THE GANGA

CLAIRE KRULIKOWSKI

Originally published by DayBue Publishing Ink

ISBN: 978-1-5040-4064-8

Distributed in 2017 by Open Road Distribution
180 Maiden Lane
New York, NY 10038
www.openroadmedia.com

*This book is dedicated to
God, our Source, Creator
who moves within us all,
that we may all feel and follow
the promptings of our soul . . .
And, also, to the creation of
heaven upon this earth
through each kind thought,
gentle, wise word,
and compassionate deed
each of us dare to live . . .*

CONTENTS

Introduction *xiii*
Awaking to the River *3*
Leave Everything You Know Behind *8*
Candles in the Wind *15*
Holy Cow *21*
Elevator Eyes *26*
Looking Another Way *34*
Conversations on the Sands of Time *56*
Cleansing Exposure *81*
Mural *88*
Seeking Higher Ground *91*
Down by the River *106*
The OM of the Cosmos *111*
Moonlight on the Ganga *115*
Thanks For What Has Been Written Before *123*
Acknowledgments *125*
Author Biography *127*

"Superficially the Ganges is just a big, slow-moving muddy stream, but if one is willing to sit upon her banks and meditate and try to absorb some of the 'soul substance' that so many hundreds of millions of people have derived from her, it is usually apparent that the Ganges is more than a mere river. Her character comes not from her superficial aspects, but from her profound inner, sacred, mystical nature and from the people who live along her banks and pass their lives in devotion to her. It is a symbolic relationship, river and people giving each other mystical sustenance."

—from *The Ganges: A Personal Encounter*, by Edward Rice

INTRODUCTION

Gaze up at the full moon some clear evening. Luminous, mysterious, mystical, her light bathes and holds us rapt in an awesome stillness, inviting us to feel her peace. So too, the sacred river of India, the Ganga; the sight of her, her mystic song, her awesome presence wakens the life of people along her banks, exhorting them to come, be near, fear not. Daring to expose your spirit to these two will unveil your own soul. I know, because I've seen my soul reflected in these.

Moonlight On The Ganga is a true accounting of surrender to the guidance of Spirit. Written throughout in journal style, this work relates some of the experiences and insights that came to puzzle and inspire me along the banks of the holy Ganga River in Rishikesh, India. Perhaps the thoughts, questions, and insights that the river churned up can be explained as easily as "if you ask it, it will come."

I had journeyed to India with several friends for the dedication ceremony of Shangri-La, an ashram gifted to an American spiritual leader, Jacqueline Snyder, by a world leader of Hindus to help further Jacqueline's spiritual work of uniting all the world's religions and people as One and help bring about the creation of heaven on earth. This gift was indeed unusual as its recipient was not only a non-Indian and a woman, but she also was not Hindu.

Have you ever done something believing you understood all the reasons for it, only to realize later that there were purposes beyond any you'd previously comprehended? I'd *believed* I was going to India to help prepare the ashram. I'd *thought* I was going in order to write articles about this fortuitous dedication ceremony, and I'd *planned* on writing the final chapters of a biography in a quiet setting. Yet, Spirit had other plans for me, and the journey to India became personally purposeful and meaningful for me in unanticipated ways as I began following the path Spirit had prepared. In doing so, I would come to own what I'd previously read about, been taught, discussed, and even felt a deep kinship to . . . but had not yet trusted enough to truly experience and live.

This work may be considered a tribute to the Ganga River, a travel memoir, and, as well, a collection of spiritual essays. The essence of it is the river, the river that flows through all time and flows through all of us everywhere; the river and its wisdom.

Beyond the physicality of anything that is described in the hieroglyphics of an alphabet and set upon its pages, all that is seen and heard and sensed is the river. It was the rising chant of these swift, holy waters and the yearnings of my own spirit that awakened my soul to how life could be lived if we let it; and so I wandered everywhere and nowhere along the Rishikesh banks for several weeks, accepting that whoever or whatever presented itself to me was there for a reason; that the clear, bright waters would raise reflecting images to show me something, would open me to more than I'd lived or imagined possible.

This book presents bite-sized vignettes of unusual personal encounters whose effects upon me link to experiences of people everywhere. These stories are easily assimilated. Whether it is drinking scalding coffee on chilled mornings, meeting a pilgrim on the sands, being sat upon by a sacred cow, painting murals, being followed by a boy with elephantiasis and a begging leper, setting candles afloat downstream, and a whirlpool of other incidents bubbling up for my notice, each ripple offered respite and reflection.

The river is instinctive, sure, and ever faithful to the essence of life. Those wisdoms carried for each of us to drink upon the Ganga waters spring from the source of its existence, which is the source of our own. Our essence continually seeks such wisdom in the journey of our many lives to realize ourselves at One with God—and all life.

Moonlight On The Ganga is a simple book of great consequence. This mystic work is essentially a tribute to the holy river of life and those of us who journey upon it. When you are in the flow, you become one with the river.

Enjoy. . . .

MOONLIGHT
ON THE GANGA

AWAKING TO THE RIVER

*"How magnificent she is when she flows in the valley of Rishikesh!
She has a blue colour like that of the ocean. The water is
extremely clear and sweet. Rich people from the plains get water
from Rishikesh. It is taken in big copper vessels to far-off places in
India."*
—Sri Swami Sivananda from *Mother Ganges*

My first sleepy-eyed morning in Rishikesh, I drink in my maiden view of the Ganga over the scalding mouth of a tall, tin cup of steaming hot Rishikesh coffee. The swift and frothy pewter river sweeping fast past me reflects the sky's overcast chill, and the instant coffee frothed with many ounces of boiled milk and sugar and something else unknown reflects nothing I've ever tasted before.

My friends and I have stumbled through the dawning day's darkness along cobble-bricked streets, weaving past bone-thin cows and their droppings, jumping over puddles of congealed water, dodging the splashed contents tossed from buckets we hope contain cleansing water for the streets rather than personal refuse from the previous evening. Clumps of cloth bundled in the street corners stir, revealing figures of bearded men slowly rising from their slumbers. There's an eerie pall of gray-brown sheathing every sight, wrapping me in the puzzling sensation of having stepped onto a movie set. Certainly this can't be real and I am not here!

We're heading to this particular chai (tea) shop at the suggestion of an American woman we met upon our late arrival at the ashram[1] the previous evening. She's lived in Rishikesh one month and tells us she has almost taught this shop owner to mix a palatable coffee. No matter, I think, it'll be tough pleasing a Seattle-latte-aholic. Her directions are easy to follow: exit out the ashram gates, down the gray marble steps, turn right onto the walkway towards the strip of stalls, and head to the second shop on the left we see that's boiling milk.

Our bodies are screaming for caffeine, screaming even louder than the amplified recorded chants and booming gongs that had been set off at 4:00 this morning, startling our bodies to leap up from the dead sleep we'd all fallen into. It had been a delayed sleep until after midnight due to our long day's drive and late arrival here. Ashram residents and townspeople had heeded that call to morning puja (prayer), but the metallic noise of that unexpected screeching had throttled our brains, causing all of our group to claw deep into our beds for any relief. We stuffed pillows, blankets, sweaters, pants, even socks over our heads in failed efforts to deafen the noise and stop the pain. We'd all breakfasted on too many aspirin before finally departing for coffee this dawn.

It's cold and windy this October morning, but we're finally up, our necks craning and turning like wild carnival rides to marvel at what may be to our right, to our left, and around the next bend. How delightful to realize we're really here, though semi-awake and no longer just dreaming of this far-off, exotic place.

Aside from the score of food merchants, as yet this morning there is only one gift shop that's thrown up its heavy metal, garage-like door to display an assortment of bright bangles and baubles and brass décor for sale. We pass without lingering, intent on our caffeine errand and knowing we'll have many days and many shops to choose from in which to spend our rupees.

Finally, we find the chai shop. Hot coffee and tea, an assort-

---

1   An ashram is a spiritual retreat center where meditation and/or teaching and lodging is available. They may each be as individual as the sage or teacher who is heading it.

ment of sodas and waters, packaged biscuits and candies, and rolls of toilet paper round out the offerings displayed over the shop's shelves. It is small, as are all the shops along this narrow alley of an uneven street, shops that were constructed many, many decades before of cement and brick with the added convenience of what must be "standard issue" garage doors. The long, endless bank of them stretching on and on along the avenue gives this pathway the appearance of an auto repair alley. Along this narrow pedestrian route, though, no cars travel.

The hawk-nosed proprietor looks less Indian to me than a resident of Brooklyn. My friends and I call out our orders for coffee in English. The proprietor is boiling milk in smudged, black pots bruised from a lifetime of bangs against two ancient kerosene burners and, no doubt, the street. His arms wave and he hollers out long strings of Hindi sounds back at us, which we just nod to.

Hoping he's understood our large order, we look around for a place to sit. Peering over his shoulder, we see four shallow plank wood tables set inside beneath a peeling ceiling. Three already host crunch-shouldered, robed, dark men whose age I cannot gauge. Beyond a narrow archway of the far wall, though, one of our band spots a curtain of gray sky. A balcony? My friends start in.

I step reluctantly into the shop, across the stained floor, and through what my U.S. bred instincts label "dank and unappealing" surroundings. Suddenly, inexplicably, though, some quirk shifts my perspective. In the States, I would have *completely* avoided *any* streets like those we've strolled and would *never* have entered into such an establishment. Yet, something in the adventure of all this is beginning to fend breeding and such concerns aside. All that matters to me right now is that I'm in the holy city of Rishikesh, and there's a chorus of water-drawn thunder—the river?—pulling me toward a whirlpool of cool, sweet air beyond the far doorway. Every seam of my nylon jacket is easy access for the bite of this morning's too brisk blast of wind.

Finally, it's my turn to step onto the narrow cement balcony. Its three waist-high walls are painted an unappealing, oily green smeared with the dirt of its age. Beyond the failing barricade of this balcony is the river whose thunderous song has been calling me.

Some of my companions have already filled the chairs at the far tables. The only other table is occupied by a solitary, sweet-faced holy man with long white hair, whose thin, angular body is housed within a many-layered robe the color of silt. A kindly smile stretches his face wide and lights his eyes, raising an answering beacon from mine. He rises, silently signaling me and those behind me, to sit. With my hands I sign a bashful "no," but he bows his head and raises his hands in prayered pose, and there can be no refusal to such hospitality.

"Namaste[2]," I say, grateful for a seat.

The table and benches are bare wood, and I throw myself onto one and skoosh to its end against the wall. From here I can poke my head over the low-slung slab wall and set my eyes upon the moving sea of life's river known far and wide as Ma Ganga, Mother Ganga, the Elixir of Life, the Sacred River, and 100 or so other attributes.[3]

Directly across this flood of fast water, which surely must be many hundred yards, sits the other half of the city of Rishikesh. The rising sun illuminates its crush of dappled temple spires, the precariously perched white square apartment buildings and brown-and-bannered-shops, all weathered by the elements to which they are exposed day after day. Upstream, draped and jeweled travelers on foot and riding ox-driven carts loaded with bundles of wood or fruits, fill the Shivanend Jhula, a steel and cement walking bridge linking the banks of this city's two halves whose single seam is the river.

The wind carries an occasional draft of urine my way from somewhere, I hope, *far* away, and returns my attention to the brackish tint of these unkempt green walls and to my friends. I've turned just in time to accept my cup of coffee from a handsome, bright-eyed boy of

2   Although *Namaste* is used as frequently as *Hello*, its translation(s) reveal the depth of spiritual consequence interactions between people can hold. Two translations I've heard are (a) "I salute the light within you where the entire universe resides, and when you are in that place within you, and I'm at that place within me, we are one." (b) "The Spirit within me respects and acknowledges the Spirit within you."
3   There are two books written in Sanskrit which can often be found in India's bazaars listing the hundreds of names prescribed to the river. They are the Gangas-tottarasata-namavali and the Ganga-sahasra-nama-stotra. These names are chanted devotionally at the river's edge and so are arranged metrically.

about nine years old who's wearing a ripped red and yellow T-shirt too small for his stretching frame. Stained, brown pants are tied around his waist with rope. He is very merry, acts much older than his age, and seems oblivious to the cold that is raising the hair on my jacketed arms.

Someone in our group has done extensive homework about India. She informs the rest of us that large stretches of the 1,550 mile-long Ganga are impassable by boat owing to plantations of boulders and sand banks planted by nature along the way, as well as fluctuating water levels that can trickle through sections of the country thick as cream-muddied oil. I swallow another long draught of coffee whose color, if not texture, matches the picture she's just painted.

She talks of the implications and controversy the building of a dam raised, and, for a second, I'm sorry for not having done more in-depth reading in preparation for the trip; but then a ribbon of chill wind curls around me, and I realize that preparation is like a thick, warm coat that would keep me from experiencing the breeze, and it's best to be free to feel whatever I feel.

My attention strays downstream to the farthest part of the western bank where dozens of buses are pulling onto the sand. They line the riverbank and release multitudes of tourists and pilgrims who've all set their personal sights on being at this river for their own individual purposes.

Far beyond them, flying low over the green-draped hillside, the huge wing-spans of four, now five, now six patient buzzards circle lazily. Their focused presence is evidence that some living thing will soon die.

Beyond anything I see or hear though, I see, hear, and sense the river. The thrusting sounds of this channel's raging waters and the imaginings of my spirit are singing tales in my ears and to my soul of how I'll wander everywhere and nowhere these next few weeks and be happy right wherever I am every moment.

In such a state of wonderment, even the ambiguous coffee begins tasting curiously appealing.

LEAVE EVERYTHING YOU KNOW BEHIND

"From the heavenly sea
The waters run and flow forward
From the never failing springs.
In my blood flow
A thousand pure springs
And vapors, and clouds
And all the waters . . ."
—from *The Essene Gospel of Peace, Book Two*
translated by Edmond Bordeaux Szekely

"Leave everything you know behind."

Mantra-like, these echoing words had swirled through my mind for weeks prior to my departure for India. The music of it had greeted me upon waking each morning, set the rhythm of my steps while strolling through stores seeking mosquito repellent, film, and handi-wipes, and its guidance helped maintain my patience while counting down the days to my departure.

Like moonlit waves listlessly rocking and caressing a darkened dock, this restful tone had lulled me to sleep each evening and carried me into the next dawning day. The song of this message, seemingly risen up from the depths of some great well, or, perhaps, a newly opened music box, haunted my steps, and I wondered what meaning it held for me.

In 1896, Mark Twain had dubbed India "The Land of Wonder." I knew India was considered a holy land, perhaps even the spiritual birthplace of the world. Yet, whenever I'd thought about India, it was images of heat, crowds, a confusion of multiple gods, and abject poverty that came to my mind. Not even the fond feelings elicited from having read *Autobiography Of A Yogi* as an eleven year old had attracted me to plan such a trip in my later years. So, wondrous as this land might be, India had never been on my Top-Ten-List-of-Places-I-Needed-to-Visit during this lifetime.

And then . . . I was going, and now I am here, and now the mantra has quieted. Prodded by that mantra in the days preceding this trip, I now realize my psyche had unconsciously released many preconceptions about the way life is or should be lived. I'm glad, because from the moment I landed in New Delhi, I haven't seen a vestige of anything I've ever known, and, as a result of leaving those rules and judgments behind, I have been able to live life more fully aware and accepting.

My first morning in India, I awoke in a grand, old, New Delhi hotel. As soon as I could ready myself, I'd headed down the winding staircase leading from my second story room to the lobby. I was intent on taking a walk around the city despite the voice of warning barking protests inside my head that I wouldn't like it and not to go.

Hooks clawed at me. Hooks of fear. Fear of poverty, disease, getting lost, the unknown, being jeered at as an American/woman/foreigner, being somewhere I didn't belong, inadvertently insulting people whose customs I didn't know. That strident voice snaked around inside me and acted as my private escort down those many carpeted steps. Yet, sunlight poured through the hotel's plate glass double doors, and I could see a wide expanse of green lawn and floral gardens fronting the property. I couldn't resist being outside.

"Leave everything you know behind," I reminded myself, and stepped outside to stand in the city's smog-strained sunlight.

I'd stepped into a world beyond time when I walked past the massive green hedges, thick-leafed palm trees, and iron gates that guarded the hotel. Many days and many miles later on this trip, I'm still happily traversing beyond all confines I'd ever placed upon people and myself prior. It all began with those first steps.

That first morning, I looked up to see flocks of massive birds crossing the sky. Their expansive wings looked the size of runner carpets. It was awesome to watch the designs they flew. A few of them landed on the tall palm trees rounding the hotel, and as they flew lower and closer, I realized these must be condors, and I was awestruck by them. Later that night, someone busted my admiration for the birds by commenting, "Big deal! Condors are just vultures." Something of the romance of those expansive wings and spiraling patterns shriveled instantly for me, and, instead, I remembered that vultures eat the dead.

Trekking the neighboring streets that first morning, many hosting consulates and embassies guarded by serious soldiers bearing serious guns, I viewed a land of ox and horse-driven carts, pedestrians, and sacred cows sharing speedway space on streets overflowing with noisy, three-wheeled motor taxis of uniform black and yellow coloring, a never ending flood of uniformly square, white minibuses, and scooters dented from daily jousting with all these others. The city avenues, thick with the rush of such an onslaught, are stretched from their prescribed two lanes to four, or even five, by the sheer determination of the drivers whose focused, free-wheeling and instinctive maneuvering gets them wherever they want to get in front of whoever is in front of them. Life surges ceaselessly around you in India whether you are ready for it or not.

On my walk that morning, I'd breathed hot air clogged with auto exhaust, and I shared the cobbled or hard dirt sidewalks with those who called them home. Some of the ample, wood-framed and corded rope-beds still hosted the resting bodies of men reading newspapers. In this land where chairs are superfluous to life, people squatted along the walkways to talk or just to wait and sit and see. The water that my U.S. Public Health Nurse had instructed me not to drink ran from sidewalk spigots where those native to this land were brushing their teeth and filling cups for refreshment. Foam frothed the faces of those being barbered at curbside, both barber and customer squatted face to face chatting Hindi while the barber's long blade scratched bristles off cheeks and chins. Taxi drivers hailed me in broken English.

"Shopping? Shopping? I take you good shops," they called out. Spending money, buying things, was the furthest thing from my mind!

In another time and in other places within the borders of the U.S., I have recoiled from scenes less foreign and as poor as these, alternately either baring my fury at the seeming injustice or shielding my emotions and mind from it behind self-erected psychic armor, refusing to hear, see, smell or taste what appalled me. Yet, here in Delhi I didn't see anything I needed protection from. It's as if I'd been released from constraints and opened to be more than just the me I'd known before. In doing that, everything around me took on a new hue and gentler feeling.

I felt more like the people I walked past on the street than not. That first morning, my eyes didn't hide from anyone. Instead, I greeted those whose homeland I was visiting and was blessed in turn to see their nobility. The beaded women squatting with their children at the water spigots wore saris that were far less becoming yet just as clean as those worn by women at our hotel. Men being lathered and shaved on the streets, whose only visible features were nose, eyes, and hair, seemed totally exposed yet comfortable within themselves. A man wearing the ragged entrails of a Western business suit sat with dignity and bearing drinking tea at a crumbling chai stand while watching steam rising from the boiling water disappear into the thick-leafed branches of overhanging tree limbs. There was no trash lining the walk or the street. Those are the people's homes, after all, and, from the look of the paraphernalia of pots, boxes, bedding, and tenting organized around them, these spots had probably been staked out by them for years or even generations.

I was not invisible to any one of them either, and, as I walked, those passing me along the alleys and roads would casually or curiously turn their wide, brown eyes onto me. Those that did always seemed quite shocked to find my eyes offering theirs a warm greeting. Something seemed to pass in that split second between us before they turned, hesitantly, away.

Have you ever been experiencing something, but felt like you were also observing, discerning its meaning, from some other place? That's how I felt that first morning in New Delhi—accepting of everything I saw and sensing something beyond the veil of what it was I was seeing, and *that* made everything okay.

I spent three days in New Delhi before coming here to Rishikesh. These memories of Delhi wash up now as I sit on a Rishikesh beach gazing upon the Ganga River.

The Ganga. This river has cast a spell over me. It speaks to me from some distant yet peaceful place about memories older than these my eyes are falling upon; a peaceful place of belief in a life that flows with ease. Some spirit sounds from it and calls me many times each day, wherever I am, to come stroll or sit near it. In those quiet moments, its long, unending strand reminds me of prayer beads, and my thoughts become prayers that finger each beaded droplet.

The river doesn't judge. The river runs. It knows no limits. Not even the outline of the land or the construction of great cities of commerce along its banks can constrain the river. I've heard stories of cities left high and dry for hundreds of years by the Ganga's sudden choice to change course. The people of many cities know that the first floors of their buildings are mere conveniences for the construction of upper floors since the first floors will flood when the Ganga overflows during the seasonal monsoons.

Today I have found a beach of monstrous boulders, thousands upon thousands of them, lodged in the sand so close to each other in places that it's easier to walk across the tops of them than step around them. And between these monstrous monoliths, the river has deposited billions of smaller "story rocks"—at least that's what I call them—because each seems to have a story to tell.

I've picked up a scarred, round, gray rock about 4 inches in diameter that's indented with symbols reminiscent of prehistoric petroglyphs. Others are purple, pink, black, assorted grays or sand-shades with swirls and lines of white or black embedded that are reminiscent of images I've seen in science fiction movies. Other rocks are opaque. A puzzle buff might go mad trying to connect all these lines that are scattered across this acreage into some semblance of a picture.

I'm sitting solitary upon one monstrous, sun-bleached oval, trying to imagine all the billions of them that are surrounding me being worn down slowly into minute granules of sand over millenniums by the pressures of time and weather. The effort is too great, though, and the call of the river mesmerizing.

I whisper the song—"Leave everything you know behind"—again and again, floating it upon the water, calling forth its meaning, sitting as long as need be to allow its hidden lyrics to rise and float to the surface.

Movement interrupts my musings and draws my attention to the right. A black mutt, about knee height with a short crown of white fur across its head and a balding backside, hops over and around assorted-sized boulders and rocks and muddy pools of congealed water left behind from the receded dam-controlled waters. The dog hops on three legs, holding the forth aloft, intent upon his quest for food. He reminds me of my Border Collie, Dash, a creature comfort dog whom I can't imagine ever surviving such a life as this one's, but still I can't despair over this wandering pooch. Instead, I watch and admire its agility for awhile before turning back to the water. Soon, however, the sound of crunching causes me to turn. The dog is pleasantly and totally fixated on chewing a long bone he's found, a meal he is eager for. I don't dare allow myself to think for more than one second about where the bone might have come from.

The river beckons again, and I turn back and allow my thoughts to ride upon the Ganga. The history and flood of her wakens and draws up the silt of memory.

"Leave everything you know behind."

This is my first trip overseas. I'm a stranger in a strange land that, everyday, has been embracing me as a friend, perhaps simply because I am not defining differences between "them" and "me." In the sight of things I had thought I would not care to see, I am seeing something beyond the mere physical manifestations that usually present themselves to third dimensional eye views.

There are memories we all carry with us that prescribe our lives—or can, if we let them. And I am now glimpsing some bulk of those that might have regimented this trip's pleasures if they hadn't been dumped! Memories of parental rules and societal rules, school rules, government rules, church rules, work rules, and history rules, all of which have ingrained in me rules about the "correct" ways to dress and live, and teach, and learn. They describe what a real house and a real stove should look like, and keep the farm animals out of the city and sick people away from the well. The rules require ownership of fine, polished furniture and the etiquette of sitting upon something called "chairs." They cast aspersions on those who relinquish worldly goods for spiritual rewards and cause people to slink away from holy men who, instead of fine robes and jeweled beads, wear nothing but a layer of ash over bare flesh. Traffic and ideas, too, are kept inside the lines.

Too, there are memories of praise and of condemnation; memories of happiness and of sadness; memories of pain and pleasures that have bulldozed the roads I've walked in my life. In the whip-like tide of this river's current, though, I feel the weight of these rules I've followed—and the ones I've not—which have brought about the praise, condemnation, happiness, sadness, pain, and pleasure that have ruled every future rule I've dutifully followed.

Watching the flood of this river is like surveying the unfoldment of my final Life Review. The chill of this water stings, the bite of long-held judgments that are chained to these rules and memories about people and places and how we and things *should* be have torn substance and joy and understanding from so many of my daily interactions and situations. There has been the "I" and "they," "we" and "them." There is "good" and "bad"; there is "right" and "wrong"; there is "my way" or "no way."

There is *another* way.

It is resistance, I realize now, that keeps things in place. I resist poverty and keep someone else poor; I resist love and always hate something or everything; I resist war and fight little wars of daily life; I refuse to trust and instead welcome fear into my life. I refuse to release some responsibility from myself and thus prevent others from taking it on for themselves. So, poverty, fear, hate, and wars—rather than compassion, understanding, trust, and love—are the established options and driving forces of life that I've recycled and reinforced every day in my daily life. Leaving everything I know behind sets me and people I meet free to set new courses.

A brand new thought tickles my awareness. I can't help wondering what would happen if I shed my memories *every day*, held no anchoring rule or expectation, and allowed myself to be always present in the flow of the river of life?

CANDLES IN THE WIND

"O brook of crystal sheen,
Could you but cause, upon your silver fine,
Suddenly to be seen
The eyes for which I pine
Which in my inmost heart my thoughts design!"
—from "Songs Between the Soul and the Bridegroom," *St. John of the Cross: The Poems,* as translated by Roy Campbell.

I have never before seen stars splashed across any sky quite like these that are grazing my head in Rishikesh. In large, industrialized cities, the incandescent lights, combined with polluted air, obscure all but the most resilient stars and leave me hungry in my skyward search. While I've gazed at the sky from my sleeping bag on isolated mountaintops in Montana and southern beaches of Mexico and seen a jazillion stars basking in the peace of the evening, only in Rishikesh do the jazillion merge upon another bajillion jazillion and seem to lay overhead thick as glittering ceiling tiles.

Perhaps they feel welcomed and called to earth by the candles and prayers of the people. For sure, the people feel called.

It is almost 6:00 p.m. I am standing upon the broad steps of the Parmarth Niketan ghat along with some hundred others. We are waiting, most standing silent, others stepping to the water's edge to say their prayers upon the Ganga, for the Aarti puja, the evening fire worship ceremony, to begin soon.

Above us, the stars have also begun gathering. Still, the young priest, wearing the orange robe of his rank, prepares. The altar is already set up at the water's edge, draped with a white cloth. Round plates overflowing with tiny marble-like candles are laid upon it, and I study the priest as he festoons each limb of the bronze tree, which will be the symbolic, physical center-piece of this ritual, with droplets of wax.

Before coming to India, I could hardly imagine taking time to pray everyday as I daily witness here. These townspeople rise before dawn to attend a 5:00 a.m. puja, and I've watched still others walk first to the water's edge to make their personal and private devotional before heading off to work and being pulled into events of daily life. During each evening, too, at Aarti puja, the ghats become the focal point all along the Ganga for prayers, for forgiveness, for creation.

Every night the stars draping the infinite sky bow low, called to earth to bless these people with jewels of light, to reflect their prayers and hold them aloft for the people of all the worlds to see. There are peoples around the world, in jungles and cities, prairies and deserts, conversing as intimately with the infinite. Perhaps we all need to leave the ceiling'd chapels behind and touch the soil, bark, leaves, streams of God's earthly flesh and allow the stars, moon, sun, the light, the wind, the fragrance of God to touch the God of our own earthly flesh. Why won't we show our face to God? It's not as though God doesn't already know what is in our hearts.

At long last, the mortal preparation of the priest is complete and immortal desires released to rise heavenward as the people begin to sing, and their voices flow as one over and upon the Ganga, the Mother whom they praise. Their words rise and fall and swoon like birds in flight, and, though I'm not schooled in the meaning of the ritual and can't this night translate the ancient words to modern text, its meaning rides currents beyond mortal sounds and sight to touch me. The priest raises and spirals the emblazoned tree high, and its wild, singular flames all erupt suddenly into one burning with faith and hope and gratitude, washing divine light upon everyone gathered within this earthly circle of people.

This procession of longing lines human cheeks with tears and calls the heavens closer to touch our flesh. I breathe in the vocal tabla[4] chorus and the river's unceasing melody, swallow the whole of the sky with my eyes, and, for a fleeting second, feel heaven within my grasp. I recollect lines from a book I once read that feel so appropriate: "Ritual means nothing if you do not know the longing that precedes it."[5]

The chorus of worship rises, and my eyes are drawn up to the heavens. Have you ever watched the sky and noticed there are some stars that blink colorful codes of green or red or blue or. . .? Ever wonder what they are? Are they really stars? What message does their light offer? I'm watching them and all the many other jiggling white ones that seem to seethe and snuggle and lie upon each other, the sky is so thick with them. Yet, still my eyes are drawn to look further, and I can peek beyond even these stellar specks. The great cosmos lies before them, between me and them. How silly, I think, to feel that greatness, that omnipotent expansiveness lies *so far out there somewhere*, and that it's such an insurmountable distance away.

"Heaven begins at your feet." Someone had told me that years ago, only now I'm beginning to understand it.

Something is calling for me to wait, and, watching these bajillion zillion specks blanketing the sky, for the first time I know that I am and have been waiting for a long time . . . as long, perhaps, as the stars have danced in the sky. And I've an odd sensation, like of one standing at a bus stop waiting for a lift, waiting . . . to be reunited.

Yet, I remain standing on the ghat, and the song of the people heralds new life, and the stem of the tree is being passed from one person to another until it comes to me, and I lift and spiral it against the silhouette of this evening. Such an awesome, potent feeling to hold a burning bush in your hands . . . but its potent power pales to that of all the prayers of the ones holding it, for these prayers rise like flames

---

4   A tabla is a percussion instrument consisting of a pair of drums. Played by hand, it adds that distinctive and fascinating sound and rhythm heard primarily in North Indian classical music.
5   Text from *A River Sutra*, by Gita Mehta, Copyright © 1993, Published by Nan A. Talese, an imprint of Doubleday.

from their hearts and souls, and the power humbles, illuminates, and enlivens.

I pass the lamp to an aged woman standing beside me and watch the flames burning in her hand. From one to another the fire is passed.

Still, their prayers chorus. Standing within the conch shell of this musical overture, I can barely hear the serenading rush of the Ganga that's running only twenty feet from where I'm standing. Its melody has always risen above the stanza of day to day life here, always sounded and resonated within some tiny chamber in the back of my mind, always made its presence known. Yet, now the people's voices crest above it, and it feels as though we're actually astride the Ganga, riding higher and higher, seeking always the highest, and, doing this, we've somehow *become* the river, and its tone become our voice and breath.

Imagine living every day as a gift, imagine remembering every day that you are part of *all* of creation. As these thoughts bubble up, my mind is flung into a quiet cove of fore and aft. There is the world *before* this trip, when my individual concerns and plans and "things to do" constrained awareness of my powers of creation and obliterated any desire "to do things" benefiting the many others. There is the world *after* arriving in India, in which I and everyone sing and ride upon the river, when daily devotions and gratitude "do things" that create gifts greater than we've yet to imagine.

I try and imagine what it will be like when people, including me, step beyond ourselves, beyond the self who cares for our self alone, and discover we've finally stepped inside who we really are only when we touch another's life.

Yet, now the final note of this evening's songs departs our lips, and the rushing call of the Ganga floods the ghat, the city, and our consciousness again. Her ceaseless tone calls an answer to every prayer, if only we will hear. The priest begins distributing the orange marigolds, which are often represented in spiritual functions here, to the people. The crowd thickens around him as everyone reaches for a flower to float their prayers upon the holy river.

I receive mine and turn to make my way through the throng. An old woman on the very outskirts of the crowd who has some type of hip or spine abnormality, is shuffling forward on stiff legs. Her long-ing for a flower and her rising panic at the possibility of not receiving one is hardening her features, maddening her eyes, and causing her to push those near her. I step beside her, break my one flower gently in two and offer one half to her. It is a simple thing I hadn't given great thought to, just done, but to watch her whole face and body calm and transform, it seemed as if some miraculous manifestation was passing from my hand to hers.

"Can it really be this easy," I wonder, "to ease another's fears, to bring happiness into another's life, to become friends with a total stranger?"

It is more than this flower we share. What passes this moment between her and me mingles, links, and transcends beliefs, cultures, flesh, fears, minds; yet, in the moment, it is fine enough to feel this ela-tion of our conjoined spirits.

We finally part from each other to take our flowers and our hearts to the water's edge. Many of the others have already gone.

My bare feet sink into water so frigid that the veins and capillaries of my feet shrivel closed in an instant, and I can hardly feel the slithery grime streaking these submerged steps I'm standing on. Any thought I'd given them disperses soon anyway as an eerie warmth fuels me, and I feel bathed in this watery womb's sweet coagulation of dark and lucent and audible delights. Around me I sense movement and hear voices passing; but, within this soft, pliable, comforting bed of water, earth, and sky I'm suddenly so aware of living within, I'm nursing liq-uid wisdoms from the river's umbilical, and feeling the shimmering lights of stars, moon, and planets revolving and dangling upon this night's celestial mobile. If I were to reach out and touch the substance of this sky with my hand, would it give and move like womb flesh, parting and flooding all below with everlasting light? There seems to be something beyond this night, this day, this place; something that is this and more; something that is growing closer, close as the stars grazing my head.

Oh, to be forever here.

The soft petals of the marigold are tickling my palm. The river's call now rises, its cadence matching the one throbbing within me. I rest my mind upon the sound like I've laid my head upon a lover's chest and draw comfort from our shared breath. It feeds me, this breath, filling me, nourishing me like no meal has ever before. This breath sustains more than my life alone.

I touch the flower to my forehead, feeding this bud my many dreams, and offer the universe thanks for this life, as well as for the more that it seems always to tease me is yet to come. Then, with a gentle toss, the marigold sets sail, and I've released the flower and all my life to the flow of the sacred river.

HOLY COW

*"Cows are considered to be sacred in India, because their milk
is symbolic of the spirit of divine motherhood, comfort, and
nurturing."*
—from *Enchantment of the World: India* by Sylvia McNair

It is noon, and for some reason, I've come to sit on the lower steps of the
ghat. I can't recall ever sitting so central and publicly placed at this time
of day. Usually I've found a haunt south on Boulder Beach or further
north on the outskirts of town. It is so busy here at noon! It's also very
hot, though, thankfully I've eaten, and, so, I'm not both hot *and* hungry.

There is something about the heat that hovers over and lays itself
upon the marble and cement and brick developments, something that
saps me of strength no matter how close to the river I sit. I have been
hot, my face even scorched one bristling day, in the more desolate or
private areas I have walked to, and yet I did not then feel this oppres-
sive weight of heat.

There is also a wall of noise and the activity of dozens and dozens
of people here washing, bathing, shaving, praying, and playing in the
water. An Italian-Hindu whom I've met previously waves to me. He's
been twirling his two-year-old son over the water and dunking him.

I decide to wait here only 15 minutes before I'll take a book into
the low hills behind me and read in the shade of the trees. Meanwhile,
I trust. Surely there is some reason I've been drawn to be here!

Turning to my right I see that at the very top of the ghat one of the street cows has managed to make her way through the lime-green gateway and is looking out from over her high place, as though surveying all our presence. She seems, oddly, like a great, infinitely patient nanny watching out for her children.

Cows have free reign in India. While in New Delhi, I'd witnessed a horde of jet-speeding cars ripping through the jammed city thoroughfares come to a screeching and seemingly impossible halt, *as one*, when a ponderous bull stepped out onto the avenue and began ambling to the center divider. No one here wants their karma affected by even an accidental injury to a sacred cow.

On this bank of Rishikesh where I am staying, the only traffic is on foot, scooter, or bicycle, so the opportunity for karmic interplay is statistically reduced; but here too, the cows roam the beaches, streets, bridges, and hillsides. Human foot traffic fends itself around these animals. My friends and I discovered early-on the danger of assuming an approaching cow would move out of *our* way. I was quicker on my feet than a couple others who suffered bruised hips and arms from their contact with the cows.

Oddly enough, there are plenty of routes these cows can take into the shade and rich greenery of the nearby mountain. In the mountains where I've hiked, I've seen plenty of them enjoying the sweet nutrition of spring nourished grasses. So, it's a sad sight to see so many cattle filling the streets of town, munching on cigarette butts, newspapers, and cardboard litter. At least it was a sad sight until someone pointed out how easily these cattle could walk up into the hills through several alleys.

"Perhaps," this man observed, "*these* cows want to be around the people."

Others thought some cows might feel comfortable and drawn by the energy of people to live in town. However, some believed that these cows had actually lost their instincts of "cow-ness."

It was a terrific discussion about free will and energy responsiveness that I'd never considered before, but I'd figured that, without hearing from the cows, it was all speculation.

Not until now, after spotting this cow on the ghat, have I realized exactly how much time I've spent talking and thinking about cows. There's been plenty.

One of the other women journeying here with me is Samantha Khury, an internationally renowned interspecies communicator. She's a gentle and effervescent woman whose presence generates warmth. I found myself standing next to Samantha on the street late one morning. Above our heads, the sun exploded over a brightly painted archway that displays the life-size statue of Arjuna[6], holding the bow given him by the fire god, Agni, with Krishna[7] handling the reins of the wild, white, running steeds pulling their chariot.

Samantha's attention was diverted by a mama cow and her calf who lumbered our way. I observed Samantha purposely maneuvering herself nearer their path and letting her hand run gently across each of the pair's backs. The cows kept walking. It was then I'd told her that I'd felt uncomfortable petting a cow earlier that same morning.

"Why?" she asked, and I had to explain my cautious desire not to insult the customs of people who consider the cows sacred. Her answer stunned me.

"I suppose it is time for us all to reconsider what sacred means," she said. "When we hold something which is alive so sacred that we do not express love towards it, how can that be considered a sacred act? I have been watching and listening to these animals. Some are so unused to attention, they are confused by the first signs of gentleness shown towards them; but, *ahhhh*, nonetheless, they still yearn for it. I think that is part of the reason for me being here. It is positioning, to bring in new energies and thoughts about this and leave an imprint here. All of these animals can feel it if you send them tender, loving thoughts."

---

6   Arjuna is considered a heroic Hindu god; one of the princely sons of the mythical (but who knows what is and is not mythical for sure) Pandu family. He's in the epic Mahabharata, which Bhagavad Gita is part.

7   The Bhagavad Gita refers to Krishna as "The Great Soul." The most lucid explanation about Krishna I've found has been in an article entitled "A Day in the life of Krishna" in the spring 1997 edition of *Parabola* Magazine: "The essence of Krishna's eternal life is enjoyment—his divine capacity to be fully present to that which gives joy . . . The highest degree of joy is attained in love—the love of a friend, a child, lover, and God."

I wasn't quite sure how or if I could communicate with animals. I wasn't sure how to conjure up pictures in my mind of love and send them to the cows, but what Samantha said about the animal's feelings touched me. From that moment on, I hadn't neglected an opportunity to pet and extend fond greetings to them. That first day, a few had even veered off their course suddenly, much to the chagrin of other people passing by, to receive a passing stroke from my hand. The first time it happened, I got excited, but then pooh-poohed it as just a co-incidence; but, when it happened again and again, I allowed myself to stay excited!

I've been getting a crick in my neck from staring up at this nut-brown cow while reminiscing about all these things. My attention has captured hers. Those big eyes of hers are glued to me! I shift my seat on the stairs a bit more so I'm facing her directly. Now I can see the extra poundage of a rounded girth—this cow is pregnant!

She's staring at me, oblivious to the people who are circuiting around her formidable bulk. Right now, to me, seeing her standing there so simply herself, the gawky frame with the trademark outcrop-pings of high and wide hip bones, her too dry and dirty fur, the fly-swatter tail, the dour skull-mask of her long face, the oddity of legs that look too thin to carry it all . . . to me they are beautiful, and she is a most wonderful and magical creature to be here making me happy just by seeing her.

She shifts her weight, causing her hoofs to click.

"Yes, you heard me," I *think* towards her. "You are beautiful, and you are a sacred cow, and your presence is an honor for everyone here."

Apparently she likes these thoughts she's hearing, because she starts making her way down the marble steps of the ghat, her hoofs *clomp, clomping* one by one, all four solidly placed in sequence upon the steps she is expertly navigating. As she makes her way down to drink from the river, I can feel what a sturdy animal she is, and she looks even finer in my eyes—until I realize with a fright that she's heading straight for *me*!

"You're a friendly one," I think when she's three arm lengths away. "You want me to pet you?" I ask. "Going to the water?" Yet, still she clomps on. Now her body's beside me. Now she's—"*Whoa!*"—standing *over* me, planting both front legs between my legs, and I'm slipping and sliding to extricate myself from any chance of becoming her butt's pillow.

She turns an expectant stare at me, and there's just no way to keep a straight face when you're looking into the eyes of a ponderous, pregnant cow waiting for her promised back rub. I stand and let my hands run along her dirt-encrusted back, her well-rounded side, which so obviously holds the protruding weight of that soon-to-be-newborn, the scruff of her fly-besieged neck, ears, and forehead. After a couple peaceful minutes, though, I figure it's time I leave. I remove my hands from her only to have the creature step gracefully, but pointedly, down onto the step I've now backed onto. Her bulk almost capsizes me.

We've captured the attention of many of those people walking across the ghat, though it's a toss-up whether our interplay or my hysterical laughter is causing everyone to stare.

"Okay, okay," I tell her, "I'll stay."

For many, many more minutes, I stroke and speak to her. Then, suddenly, images, thoughts of her calf flash into my head! This cow hasn't just come for herself. She's come because she wants her calf to sense this pleasure, this love being received from a human being. This mama is standing placidly in the noon day heat accepting all I can offer her and her child, and there's no containing my tears and the joy I feel communing with her in this tender way.

Close to one hour later, my hands thick with tar-like grime and the dry stubble of shed fur, my arms and back long weary, the three of us say our good-byes. I hug the thick neck of this mystic mother, who, everyday in her bovine way, does what needs doing without complaint and who senses more than many humans allow themselves to feel.

I step back, allowing her ample room to roam. She bows her head and raises it, acknowledging, it seems, satisfaction and appreciation with what has passed between us. Then this mother continues plodding down the marble steps, but I don't—I can't—watch her go. Instead, I hurry to leave, hurry to find my hillside hideaway where I can sit alone and cry and feel all the love she's offered to me.

ELEVATOR EYES

"The thought came to me: 'Be water. Be water. When you can be water, you will find water.'"
—from *Mutant Message Down Under* by Marlo Morgan

It is a very different experience to visit India intent on depositing love, understanding, and joy rather than journeying to seek those things.

Morning, noon, or night, I walk the well-worn lanes around Rishikesh. Sometimes I go to town on an errand to buy soda, which is contraband in the ashram where I am staying, or I go to sip the odd tasting coffee. Most times, though, the pleasures that draw me into the busy town of Rishikesh itself are the glimmering, fine gemstones that dance around me there.

The gems that so dazzle me are not displayed within polished glass casements, though. Neither is the treasure bankable within the confines of stores and vaults, nor do foreigners often get to see them. The gems that light up my life are the eyes of the people I meet or pass in the street. Their delight is shared with me every time I offer mine to them. A warm smile of greeting creates incomprehensible wealth.

As a whole and historically, the relationship of Western people with the people of India has not been one of overt friendliness, egalitarianism, or mutual respect. Despite this, the native Indian people eagerly receive and return appreciation with effervescence. In the course of a couple weeks, the town has become alive with bright eyes seeking out mine. The school children whom I've watched daily parading the streets in single file to and from school, accompanied by their teachers, have begun jumping up and down, waving, singing, and calling to me saying "hi, hi." Sometimes an instinct has caused me to look over my shoulder only to discover that the person I've just greeted and passed is casting curious looks back at me. Every day, I've experienced this. Without conscious plan or effort on my part, in a rhythm that is as natural, now, as breathing, my eyes have sought out the orbs of the persons approaching me, pouring my greeting, interest, and love for them into *their* initially surprised or suspicious gaze. The eyes are said to be the mirror of the soul, after all.

"Namaste," I say, folding my hands in prayer, all the while continuing moving forward, and within split seconds I catch the warmth exploding from their soul's eyes like brilliant light dancing off fine jewels.

Verbiage isn't what connects people, I am learning. I am learning to communicate in new ways.

This day I've had to stop and sit on a cement bench in the colorful, overflowing garden of one of the ashrams. I'm sitting because the sky has called me here. Not the sky exactly but what's being written upon it. Wisps of clouds, like strands of ribbons, are lining themselves across the otherwise blue sky and beginning to scroll a design of foreign letters into some language I can't translate.

I'd seen the calligraphy begin, though no one else seems to have noticed, which is amazing! Am I hallucinating? No, I *see it*. I wonder what language this might be. Could it be the ancient Sanskrit, and if so, what are the Holy Ones trying to communicate to us mortals below? I have to sit. I don't know why, but I've got to sit.

An overflow of leafy palms and prismatic floral bushes surround me. Their intense scents mix with the aroma of the lush mountains, and I'm overcome by the ambrosia-like blend of honeysuckle, hyacinth, pine, roses, and a plethora of other aromas. Around the courtyard are statues of various gods and carved statues depicting scenes from ancient, sacred texts. Visiting Indian families are strolling excitedly from one to another, and there's plenty of chatter from wide-eyed children.

My attention returns to the heavenly papyrus. The words are still hanging there. Still, no one else seems to notice. Why do I believe I'm really seeing this?

Seek and you shall find. Someone is coming.

A middle-aged Indian woman with bone-thin features, her movements as delicate and quick as a robin, shuffles towards me. Her eyes call mine to look at her. Her hair is black and heavily spackled with gray. A tarnished gray shawl hangs over her rounded shoulders and covers the faded green sari she's wearing. Her thin left arm doesn't seem wrapped with enough muscle to bear the weight of even the green and beaded bag that weighs it down. The paper-thin soles of her blue, rubber "flip-flops," a common footwear here, creates the scraping and shuffling sounds she makes when walking. She bows up and down, up and down, up and down, as she approaches me, her smile so wide it seems tied to both ears, her eyes rising and dipping like ship lanterns signaling greetings to the shore.

"Hari Om,"[8] she greets me reverently.

"Namaste," I answer. Instead of passing me by, she stops to carefully place and lift one foot and then another up and down, turns again and lifts them up and down again, and finally again. This brings her full circle with her palms open and bowing again, before she finally sits on the bench next to me. It seemed quite a ceremony in its way.

I try to talk with her, but my first couple sentences verify that she understands no English. That doesn't disconnect us.

"Beautiful," I communicate by opening my arms to the gardens.

"Yes," she agrees with a beaming, baby-like smile.

Are we really going to communicate without words? I begin asking her questions in my mind and pass these thoughts to her.

"Does she come here often?"

Her eyes smile, her eyebrows raise, her hand touches her heart, and I understand, "Yes."

---

8   A common greeting in India, which again illustrates the depth of simple interactions. "Hari" can be an expression of God; "Om" (or Aum), is considered the primordial sound or the original vibration of the universe. So, being greeted with "Hari Om" sets you up for a heavenly day!

I also come to know, as we continue to laugh together and speak an unspoken dialogue, that she lives in town, on the other side of the river, and that she will be at this ashram for the morning Puja. I think she is asking me if I can go. I shake my head and say verbally, "No, I have not yet been."

She tilts her head, her eyes quiet, and she waits for me. I have spoken a different language. Moments pass. When I finally acquiesce in thought, she knows it before I even verbalize "Yes, I will be there," and she is wiggling with joy. She confirms, without words in her way, that she will be there also. It appears I have made a pact, and one she is happy about.

The woman rises, bowing again and again, "Hari Om, Hari Om," and I bow continuously to her also until she rounds the greenery draped gate and disappears from sight.

The spell begins to dissipate and lift like fog rising over a lake, and I try to understand what's just transpired between us.

"What sort of telepathy has this been?" I wonder, but I don't understand it. Finally, confusion miring my mood, I turn to read the sky's scroll again.

It's gone! Erased!

"Whoa!" The magic of life appears by invitation, I realize, and has to be first accepted before received. What gifts I've received, but . . . why? What does it mean? Perhaps I need to be even more attentive today?

I feel an urge to walk into town.

The vendor-lined boulevard is always bustling this time of day. A group of people is stopped at two wooden carts heaped high with mounds of cucumber, cauliflower, bananas, and oranges. The people are all pointing and lifting and gesturing at the proprietor who is busy listening to everyone at once and doing only one thing at a time. I've done business with this man. He does not haggle over the price of food, at least not with foreigners. The scale he weighs the foods on is his law. Money and food are exchanged between him and the customer, and it is a straight-forward, busy business.

Tunes of bamboo flutes and tablas rise from somewhere unseen in the crowd ahead. Sound, as everything else of life, is believed here to be a divine gift of Brahma, Lord of all Creation. Colors and moods continuously ascend and descend on the raga melody and set my mind wandering like my steps, unsure where I'll stop or why. This morning seems too beautiful a day to squander in the busy-ness of this commerce. Yet I feel something old is becoming new. It feels as if some secret will be revealing itself, and I'm urged forward.

I greet those I pass, and their return greeting, as usual, makes me feel very open and pleased to be here. Now, though, very obvious among the dark Indian crowd, two blond Anglos, a man and a woman, are approaching wearing blue jeans and beige short-sleeved shirts. Suddenly, I'm very excited at the prospect of meeting people of a culture I am more familiar with and imagine us sharing stories about India over tea, and so I look expectantly at them the whole time.

Their eyes eventually connect with mine, swiftly look down, and they continue to walk and pass me by without offering any greeting.

I've been rejected! Why?

It takes a minute before I realize that this is nothing new. I've witnessed this every day in my wanderings without letting it "register." It had discomforted me, but I'd always let it drop because I'd been so focused on the other things going on around me. Now, though, I'm puzzled and wonder what this means.

I spend my next hour on the strip observing "foreigners" from Germany, or perhaps, America, Sweden, France or England. I notice they act distant from everyone else around them. None of them make any effort to link with me. No crystals sparkle in their eyes as have exploded in the jewels of the Indians. No, instead, when I try to connect with the other Americans and Europeans, their "elevator eyes" drop or turn away. Instead of greeting me, or even the townspeople, their vision is masked to all except cow dung, their companion, or the trinkets lying in display cases.

What is this separation about? As usual, my question leads me to the river, and I walk down the steps of one of the many ghats and settle myself on a sunny, dry spot, free of litter and dung.

Three children are playing and splashing in the water, sternly supervised by a mother intent on having them wash instead. Two bristly-haired, beige dogs trot down the steps past me, noses never long off the ground of continual temptation where whiffs only a dog could love might lead to tasty morsels. One of them turns and stands next to me. There is nothing stereotypically miserable about *these* animals. They are alert, and this one's golden brown tiger's eyes leap here and there along the bank, to me, across to the distant shore, and then into the sky to follow the path of a darting bird. My hand almost moves to pet this delightful, wiry guy, but the scolding I'd received in the U.S. about the lack of rabies vaccinations in India from my doctor ("When you're over there, if you see anything cute, furry, and *ever so* pet-able . . . *don't!*") keeps my hand resting on my lap. The warning can't stop me from talking to him though.

"Hi, guy," I say. Oh, when he turns those golden eyes of his towards me, I melt! I tell him where I am from, and how smart and charming he appears. He must like what I have to say because he starts telling me quite a story in a fit of whines and whistles and powerhouse yawns. Even the dog will talk to me!

I nod understanding to him (I don't really, but it would be rude to ask him to repeat himself!) and tell him about my three dogs and how I'd saved them from being on the street, and how much I miss them. Then I ask him if he knows he's living in one of the most sacred cities of India and does he feel special?

Yes, he already knows that, is what I understand from his single bark. Apparently he likes it here beside me, or he's bored with the intellectual level of my conversation, because he pants in my face a few times before settling down to sleep beside me. As he closes his eyes, I wonder if somehow he's been sent as a sort of messenger from—or for?—my dogs. Are they sending me a dog to feel close to, or will this one commune back with them about how I'm doing?[9]

With my companion sound asleep beside me, I relax and let my

---

9   On my return to Washington, one of the first stories I heard was how, one afternoon, a tiny Pomeranian appeared in the driveway of my home. My friend, who was home, scooped it up and brought this pooch into the backyard—a normally dangerous act due to my dogs' territorial instincts. Guess what? That Pomeranian licked all the dogs' faces, and they all played quite well together for several hours. Eventually, a visiting "out of state" couple came searching for their lost dog. Obviously, to me, my dogs had also been sent a companion to keep them company for awhile. Hmmm. . . .

mind retrace the paths I've walked today. I see, again, those Anglo eyes stray from mine, but now it's the feelings that pressed against me as they'd passed me that are speaking louder now that I'm listening to hear their truth. It feels as if these people were embarrassed to meet me because I reminded them of a world they'd left behind in order to find something different or better here. Or, more exactly, perhaps with some, they have come here seeking spiritual growth from the great— and not so great—teachers residing in Rishikesh, and I am viewed and judged a mere tourist, and the townspeople as residents who have nothing to offer them. In any case, the separation is real, and it is of their own, probably unconscious, fabrication. Sadly, it continues in this little town as a microcosm of the cycle of separation and dualism evident between people in cities and towns worldwide.

"Where is their heart?" I wonder.

The river flows before me, speaking another truth. Any teacher who is truly great knows, lives, and teaches Oneness. Any "student" who acts as One, rather than merely quoting or aspiring to it, is a great teacher.

I let the streaming river reflect a new lesson to me about the dance between people. I notice how the river reflects the weather of the sky. A gunmetal sky darkens and chills the appearance and bod- ing of the water it looks down on, sending a shiver through the spirit and blood of those who allow its intensity to infiltrate their life. Yet, the river shimmers blue and clear, bright and sparkling under the light of a brilliant blue, sunlit sky, and there are many varying hues in between. So it is that what people reflect outward by our beliefs, thoughts, words, and deeds color our world and the lives of those we meet.

"How do I paint my days?" I wonder. What play of light and shadow dances across the screen of my every interaction? What colors are reflected back over my life by other members of the cast?

How will I behave and live when I return home? India is allowing me to be different than the way I am at home. For some reason, an intensity, a distrust, a fear that's ruled me for years has calmed here. What will happen when I return home to a land that is less tradition- ally attuned to, or even tolerant of, Spirit—A land where fear and those societal rules I've left behind keep eyes downcast and people separate from each other?

On my return flight, will I just as eagerly and easily greet the people I meet in the crowded Hong Kong and San Francisco and Seattle airports as I have along this Rishikesh strand? In my hometown, will I share unspoken greetings with my bank teller as happened at the ashram between the green sari'd woman and me today? How will all of my relationships be affected by what I am coming to know here? Will I just forget it all and return to the routines of habit and socialization and "the way things just are?"

I hope my experience in Rishikesh doesn't become just like a fad diet for me. It's hard to swallow the thought of returning to that other lifestyle that now seems so bland and hurtful in comparison to the sweet riches unveiled to me here.

It's magical to feel this happy. I feel like a child riding a magic carpet over clear, luminous water in a flight from the heavens to the sea. Experiencing this sense of divinity won't be easy to give up!

I suspect I'll be reminded by the pains of that other life when I'm not acting this peacefully. Do you remember experiences as a child, like running into the house all elated and happy from a day of playing, only to be met with stern words and harsh glares from parents who'd been busily engrossed in other kinds of games that hadn't left them feeling quite so good and happy?

So, I suspect I'll know when I'm not feeling as good as this. I suspect I'll find the gems back home when I cast a different light upon the life I live there.

LOOKING ANOTHER WAY

"The truth takes flesh in forms that cannot express it; and thus its history and ideal always overhangs, like the moon, and rules the tide which rises simultaneously in all the souls of a generation."
—Ralph W. Emerson from *On God and Man*

Back home there is a grove of cedar trees in my half-acre yard within which circle I sit and meditate in the crisp clarity or the mystic myth of early morn. I feel it is a place very much alive with creatures seen and unseen. Crystal light pours from the morning sun down through profuse terraces of cedar limbs. The rays of light glisten off dainty dew drops draping every doily-like leaf. The first morning I stepped into the grove's circle was a birthing moment that still raises chills—a moment when magic and the existence of things not easily explained, junctions between other realities, filtered like that filament through fissures in my awareness.

The point of these musings is that the wonder called me, and I accepted its invitation to sit there. Here in Rishikesh I am daily, each minute it seems, feeling beckoned off some beaten track of tasks I might set myself to do. I'm seeing what would be perfectly ordinary sights from other-ordinary angles and perspectives. Here, too, some 20,000 frequent flyer miles away from home, there is an unseen force or energy opening windows for me to gaze beyond. Something is slipping opportunities like moonbeams through apertures between my beliefs.

What kinship leads me to meet people and think such thoughts as I have been these many days in this foreign land? These thoughts, insights, and people have been trailing and fluttering around me like gay party banners or Indian sutras.[10] Only, today is much less gay than other days have been. I'm aware enough to know that what I see is meant somehow for me, but what dream am I today waking to?

The Plea

Feeling corralled within the town, I have walked many miles today, but my amble has not been pleasant. I've spent most of the day looking down rather than up. Vendors have pleaded with me, snake charmers hissed at me, and for the first time since leaving New Delhi, insistent children groped and tugged for my attention and coins. It's been a bothersome few hours. I'd thought, when setting off this early morning, that I was just going for a walk to get away from the growing familiarity and weariness of the town. I'm finding more than I'd bargained for and far less peace than I'd hoped. I don't know to what degree the surroundings have affected me this way, or how I may be drawing such experiences my way. Three-quarters of the way back, I'm too tired to think anymore. Instead, I just concentrate on placing one foot in front of the other, knowing that no matter what or why, I've collected a trunk full of memories today.

It has been a hot, sweaty, exhausting few hours of walking winding, dusty roadways, all the while alert and dodging streams of marauding tin cans—called taxis—that usurp every inch of a narrow road's width. I've only taken a few breaks, either to buy a warm cola at a shop half the size of my home's hall closet, or to explore for buried treasure amidst dirt-blanketed crystals hidden in the darkness of a hillside shop that looks more like a cave.

---

10   When the original Indian scripts of knowledge were eventually placed in writing (and please remember that India is rich in *oral* tradition), they were written on palm leaves and tree bark with a stylus dipped in ink. Displayed together hanging on a cord, the holy texts came to be called *sutras*, or, cords.

I have no idea of even the names of the towns I'm passing through. Are they each a suburb of the other, or are they distinct abodes with individual names and histories? Except for the differentiating presence in the town squares of an occasional fountain or shrine carved to honor Shiva or another deity, one place seems very much twin to wherever I've been before.

Round and round, and up and down I go, over hill and across dale, forever besieged by masses of people. I continue onto narrow bridges dangling over water which link lands which no longer naturally desire to be linked; then, I follow highways only to double-back into an alley when some instinct tells me that particular roadway won't return me to the comforts of my Rishikesh ashram.

How funny! Concepts like "comforts" and "ashram" used in the same sentence had seemed an oxymoron when I'd first arrived, at least in Western terms. I am now well aware how good I have it where I'm staying. Unlike many of the citizens of Rishikesh, my room has a water heater and hot and cold running faucets, plus a wool blanket for warmth. The inch-thick cloth mattress they've also supplied me with undoubtedly softens the experience the plank board would have offered. Yet after today's long trek, as the familiar spires and squares of Rishikesh leak into view beyond the trees and failing structures that look like stage props, my leg and back muscles are *screaming* to lounge peacefully on a comfortable, thick, Queen-sized mattress resting over cushioning box springs.

I can't take another step. My body's engine sputters to a halt just outside of Rishikesh on a strip of land that kneels against the Ganga. In the distance, there are stick figures heading to and from town, but no one is nearby to intrude or distract me from my rest.

I pull off my shoes and socks and step into the cold river, letting the soles of my feet sink and languish in the soft, sandy ooze. My hands pluck water from the stream and toss those cool drops of Ganga petals on my brow, over my head, and across the back of my neck. God, it's hot!

I lie back on the pebble-strewn dirt. Sleep pulls me. My mind begins wandering, and some fantasy flings me to the isle of Maui where I've just pulled my rental car off the road to enjoy the quiet of a deserted stretch of beach. The roll and ripple of tiny waves coax me to deeper and deeper sleep. Such fantasies are dreams made of. . . .

A clatter of stones nudges my consciousness, but not enough to fully wake me. More clatter and tumbling. A cough.

"What kind of dream is this?" I wonder, yawning, seeking a return again to sleep.

Another cough. Suddenly, a primitive instinct bolts me upright, abruptly aware and fearful of my exposure here as a lone female.

Behind me, off to the right and, perhaps, twelve feet away, a ragged-haired man swathed in the typically clean, robe-like clothing males here wear, leans upon a crooked stick twice his crumpled size. It's impossible to tell whether the Shar Pei-like facial folds express or disguise his true character. What can't be read through them may just be my projection.

He has been waiting patiently for me apparently, but such quiet respect has its anticipatory limits, and before I can blink twice, he is mumbling something completely incoherent and weaving expressive, ribbon-like designs in the air with his hands to accentuate whatever plea he is making. Surely the downcast face and droning call beseech me for something.

I shake my head. "I'm sorry. I do not understand."

Whatever his need, it is surely more than alms; upraised palms would signal that easily enough. What story is this man trying to tell me? I settle myself into an almost Zen-like pose. His voice drones on like a horde of bees busy within a hive.

I want to understand but cannot catch even one familiar syllable and wait patiently, leaning into the sounds he's making. This pivoted attention silences him, and he assesses me with the cocked and guileless expression of a curious babe. Now we are both equally attentive to each other. Will this make a difference?

His dull eyes implore me. In another second he resumes his staccato. This time though, he speaks much slower and more sorrowfully, which allows what sounds like "duck tour" to release from the bundled yarn of mixed verbiage.

"Doctor?" I ask.

Relief washes his limp skin even as new excitement tumbles another avalanche of speech my way. A headache creeps up my neck and strangles my skull. My brain feels squeezed dry. It's been a long, tiring day.

I hold up my hand, which stills him. I request that he sit by patting the ground. He glances around and finally eases himself onto a decaying log that's set amidst the jumble of boulders, sticks, and stones separating him from me.

My right hand lays over my heart.

"What do you need?" I ask him. It is not enough for me to already know that, bottom-line, it is bound to be money. I've only a two rupee note[11] left in my pants pocket, and that will buy him nothing at all. There is something more this man needs to tell me.

Perhaps because he senses my willingness to listen, he is calmer now. More words tumble forward. "Calcutta" and "duck tour" and a new word like "gut" are the only syllables I can make out. Meanwhile, his hands are scuttled deep inside the folds of cloth enveloping his body, and they finally extract a two-inch square of beige paper. He raises himself up, takes a step balanced on his stick, and leans forward waving the slip for me to take. He chatters on, and I decide to meet him half way. My hand almost closes over the paper when a warning within my brain says "leave it," but I choose to not listen and take the squared sheet over to a boulder to read.

The sheet is worn smooth as wax from much handling and refolding. I unfold the sheet and suddenly feel thrown someplace far, far away where I am contemplating the ragged edges of the courier font rather than the meaning of this note which informs "all who read this" that this man's leprosy requires care in Calcutta at a cost of approximately $1,000.00.

Indeed. Gut = Cut. Apparently, this note is meant to convince me that roughly 35,000 rupees will spare him that.

From the distant vantage point where my consciousness has run

11   At an exchange rate (during the time of my trip) of approximately 35 rupees per dollar, two rupees doesn't get you much of anything in India. Depending on where I was, for example, bottled water cost from eight to 25 rupees.

for safety, mental alarms are ringing out The-Little-I-Know-About-Leprosy-Facts-And-Myths-Unbounded.

Mind chatter: "No!, No! No! What have I done? Is it contagious? What'll happen to my hand? Don't touch anything else! Am I contaminated? Isn't there a shot you can get? It doesn't seem to have helped him. *I gotta get outa here!*"

My eyes, not able to believe what they're reading, are still watching my hands holding the silky sheaf. A voice that's not mine whispers a reminder inside my head: "Isn't there always more to see?"

Careful to avoid eye contact with this man, I choke back panic and reconnoiter my sights across the stubbled earth, above the treescape to gaze upon the teal blue sky where a single, tall cloud, proud and sure as a stallion, rides across the heavens. I watch its strong, even gait for a long time and find myself reminiscing how, as a child, I used to lie in the grass of my yard and imagine myself riding wild horses across mountainous clouds that ranged *sooooo* high in the sky.

"Don't fear," the spurred cloud seems to whisper. I try not to, but my body feels hard and heavy as lead.

I refold the paper and hand it back to the man who is sitting, waiting quietly for my help. I note the gray overcast set to his eyes. It's such an odd color rarely seen in this culture. But, maybe it's odder that I'm looking into them.

I shake my head "no." He stands and pulls back his robe from his leg, revealing the stump of his left leg, toes eaten clean off, patches of charred dry skin pocking the remains of this driftwood-like appendage. A defensive part of my mind screams "scam" and plays out scenes of this man's begging reaping a bounty for his family, but the torch of my heart burns that film to cinder. How can I look at that decayed flesh and judge this man! It isn't that easy for me anymore to callously erase the suffering of this single human being even if available medication may have already controlled his disease.

I point towards the town, feeling the uselessness of the question, but needing to ask anyway.

"Town. Rishikesh. Hospital. You go?"

Wrong question.

"Cut. Cut." His wire-thin hand slices at his knee. "Calcutta . . ." he begins and is off again upon a firebrand of an explanation that is totally wasted on me since I don't understand a word. He is trying to tell me there are treatments available in Calcutta that the doctors in Rishikesh centers do not offer. I can't necessarily believe that this holy city is less humanitarian than Calcutta, but he probably knows more than I do.

I look at him and see everyone I've *ever* seen in need. I look at his ravaged leg. I try to envision what his life must be like, and I know it is utterly impossible for me to do anything beneficial for this man right here, right now. He chatters on, and I set my sights elsewhere, trying to find a vantage point to clarify what I'm experiencing.

No amount of money I can give him will really change what I am seeing. No words I speak are going to cure him either. So what has brought us together?

It's hard to think when your brain's cemented shut by exhaustion and sights rather left unseen.

I stare at him and discover that my silence has apparently quieted him as well. He is depressingly idle, his frame slouched and depleted of all form and substance, his eyes rolling from scene to scene around us the wayward way a marble might roll listlessly from one point of contact to another.

I think of the many different kinds of people all over the world and the many ways people live and prosper and just survive. In the cycle of reincarnation, what is it that brings this man to choose this place and this way to live? Why choose to physically deteriorate in India instead of, for example, selecting a suburban life in Los Angeles? Or, if this isn't exactly what he'd planned for this lifetime during his heavenly life between incarnations, what choices had he made during this life that led him to where he is now?

What about me? Why do I do what I do? Someone driving a swanky new car past me in my home town, or someone who's felt a stirring of righteousness in their breast, might question the choices I've selected. Another person might envy me. What good does judging do? Surely there are more soul empowering forces at work than we might know or admit.

Now the Ganga seems to be the focal point of his stare, and he seems to be smiling. It is good to see. Still, this man's wounds, physical and otherwise, need healing. Doesn't everyone's? Is that one of the many metaphoric lessons this man's life represents to me right now? Is the birthing of pure spiritual living actually dependent upon each of us caring for each other? Is that the point when we grasp the full girth of our soul?

Can love actually, *truly* heal on a more potent level than merely physical? Does it cure as potently as hate and stress kill? In the fulfillment of my life's happiness, is this man affected positively somehow? Are the dreams of an individual really already swirling within the realization of the plans and dreams of all of us individually? Does one person's conscious success in healing make it easier for another?

The man is pointing at his leg again, imploring me with outstretched arms. I shake my head. "I am sorry. I cannot help you in that way."

He speaks. I say no. He talks more. Another "no" fails to thwart his flood of pleas. I shake my head. Unlike years ago, though, when I would have gotten angry and closed my heart and my mind to his existence, to his persistence, when his condition was a threat or challenge of some sort to who or what I was and all that I had accumulated . . . now I care in a way that doesn't doom me to suffering, to guilt, to anguish, to fear; and, the whole while my head turns right and left for "no," I am also silently praying for his good health and envisioning him just a little stronger than he believes himself to be.

It is impossible to reject him, abandon him, because in other ways and at other times, I've felt something of what he does: abandonment, fear, pain, helplessness, poverty, rejection, horror, exhaustion, loneliness, hopelessness. This man's looking-glass eyes reflect simple human needs in a world where I know there is enough wealth to provide it, though it has yet to be freed up for the betterment of him and many others. When hearts open, the coffers will also I suppose, but the healing begins in the heart.

Memories coalesce of what it's felt like when a harsh word or turn of the head answered my pleas. Like a hammer striking flesh, some piece of me had felt pained, then numbed, then deadened, if even only just for a moment. Imagine a life spent fending off hammer blows? This man's flesh is so deadened, it's falling off.

Desperate for my attention, he renews his effort and raises his voice in a shrill appeal. My silent prayer, spoken in a language, a vibration, he's too preoccupied right now to hear, goes unnoticed. No matter. Perhaps it will take more potent form some night in a dream. Meanwhile, he goes on, his features reeking sorrow. A long spell of this will do neither of us good, so I finally speak my heart.

"Sir." He does not hear. "Sir."

He stills.

"I cannot do anything for you; not physically, and I am sorry because I want to. Believe me, I wish you health and peace."

And I salute him with prayer-clasped hands.

Probably none of these English words have been understood by him, but the gesture is one that means much more to people of this land, and he quiets and also bows his head. It is then I hand him the wrinkled two rupees from my pocket. If only it were more.

I finally turn away when it feels not disrespectful to do so.

In less than a minute, I hear behind me the soft clatter of tumbling stones marking his departure. I allow plenty of time before turning back to watch him leave. His caned-pace is steady and less awkward than I'd have thought possible given the banked and rugged soil, and his solitary figure grows smaller and smaller at an even speed. How many strangers does he meet upon these banks each day?

The Prayer

Before I can turn back to the river, I spot several groups of people strolling my way. There is a single man, and, behind him, two men. Further back I think there are two teenaged boys.

I'm suddenly bone weary. The hours of walking through villages, being pressed for attention, the sight along the way of so much need, the weary horses, skeletal cows, and hobo dogs, and all the time feeling the unexpressed, perhaps unrecognized need for fulfillment surrounding everything has taken its toll. I need silence. The thought of any more interaction, the need for any more thinking, the feeling of any more emotion is more than I can take. I decide to ignore this parade of people. Perhaps, though, it's not appropriate for me to ask that since my stay here seems guided by other forces? Perhaps there is need of agreement about this? I ask for assistance.

"God, please," I sigh. "I'm tired. I've had more than I can handle right now. Is it possible to please keep any people away who do not have something uplifting and *positive* to show me? I just need some quiet right now."

Well, no harm asking. *Now* I feel comfortable enough to turn my back and focus on the sound, sight, and smell of the water again, though my every sense remains alert for "intruders."

A furtive glance catches sight of the first man suddenly turning back as if he'd lost something. I relax and begin writing again.

Now I sense and then hear the duo closing in . . . passing behind, and. . . . Yes! They're walking past me. What a sigh of relief! I allow myself to forget about the kids. My prayer is being answered!

At least I thought so; but moments later, here they are, thirty feet away, two long-limbed teenage boys running barefoot in and out of the water for no apparent reason other than frivolity. One is trying his best to drench the other, who is doing *his* best to keep a notebook clenched safely in one hand. My every muscle tenses. I just *know* they're going to start hassling me like typical schoolyard wise guys or subway bullies or . . . or insistent Indian street kids determined to shake down a foreigner!

Now fear wallops my guts! Suddenly this strip of isolated land feels treacherous as a razor's edge, and somewhere on an inner island of my psyche, beyond the fear, I'm also registering that this is the first time I've been angry and afraid since arriving in India—the very first time!

There's no more time to think about that though. One kid pokes the other and points my way. Oh, no. Here it comes! They run over.

"Miss, miss."

I pretend not to hear them. I dig my pen hard into the paper, scratching messages so the police will know what's happened ("Two teenage boys, thin, black pants, bare-chested, brown-skinned, black hair, wide smiles"—*Oh, good Claire, that's distinctive in India!*—"About five foot, two inches and five foot, four inches. They're surrounding me. Help!").

My note is small comfort to me. What are the chances that, if I suddenly disappear or am found dead, some English-reading person will happen to walk this way some day *ever* and discover the, probably by then, monsoon-drenched journal? What are the chances it won't be considered just beach trash but something worth turning into the Lost and Found (in India?) of the local Rishikesh police force and that they'll at least discover what happened to me? Yeah, right!

A huge shadow creeps over the page I'm staring at.

"Oh, Miss?"

Draw deep breath. Release breath. Grip pen like knife. I'll go down fighting. Turn. Look up.

His hand stabs towards me. "Pen? Write? Me borrow?"

He's smiling . . . and I'm feeling like a jerk—a very relieved jerk trying desperately to breath again while fumbling for the spare pen in my pocket. But, caution grips me again!

"It's a trick," I think, and I flex my knees, ready to make a desperate escape, but I hear his pal's feet kicking stones behind me. I'm surrounded! I brace myself and hold the pen out to him.

He grabs it. "Thank you."

He runs. His pal joins him. Together, these two leap over boulders and a dry log rotting on the sand. They sit down and start talking and laughing and writing in the book they'd brought.

It takes a few unblinking minutes before my old fears disintegrate, and when they do, laughter rips my every taunt muscles free, scatters those old memories upon the wind, and sends tears of relief streaming down my cheeks.

Oh, man! What have I done? I'd just turned a couple carefree kids into horror movie ax murderers! *Where* on earth has this erupted from? I don't even *watch* scary movies!

Sometimes fear can rise up, overtake you, and turn wherever you are into a living hell. Thank God I hadn't taken off screaming! What a mad woman I'd have appeared!

The boys are giggling and scribbling while running along the sand, elbows jostling the other's, each in turn stealing the pen back from the other, oblivious to me and all else except the game they're enjoying. They sure as heck aren't concerned or worrying about me. This time my pen is the prize, and it's great to watch their quickness and light-hearted dance of advance, retreat, circle, dive; to see the sand they kick up; to hear the wild abandon of their abundant laughs tossed so high and free into the air.

Finally, one exhausted lad trips and falls, panting hard, and sur-renders to the taller one who is jubilantly carrying and waving the pen and book! Good friends still, the one helps the other up and they both pound each other ceremonially on the back. Then they run back to me, returning my pen with many happy thanks, and continue walking onto wherever they were going, laughing the whole way.

It's been a delightful few minutes of carefree entertainment, mixed with a bit of wisdom about the release of harbored fears. I'm resusci-tated enough to head back to the ashram. I slap dried dirt off my feet and pull on socks and shoes. My earlier prayer sprints to mind. All in all, this meeting has qualified as a positive one even if in unexpected ways!

The Unforgiving

I know something's wrong as soon as I open the door.

"Why is nothing going right?" I grumble.

Clothes are knocked off the shelf, and the bag of bananas that was set there is torn to pieces. Discarded peels from the dozen are scat-tered over my blanket and strewn across the floor along with trash from an overturned garbage can. Orange rind remnants litter my roommate's bed. Either my fun-loving roomie has developed odd eat-ing habits or the monkeys have found entry. Hard to believe, but I vote for the monkeys!

These ashram rooms are constructed with a three-foot by two-foot hole set in the ceilings and floors. Long-term residents at the ashram cook in their rooms, and these apertures offer needed ven-tilation for the portable kerosene burners they bring with them. It hadn't dawned on us that these gaping holes would also serve as entryways for the monkeys who wander freely over the surrounding hills and every rooftop. Indeed, we've lived sublimely until now. So this must be perfect timing—perfectly ripe bananas and perfectly punctual monkeys.

This clean-up seems more like comic relief!

Afterwards, a quick shower and a nap relieve my exhaustion. Shadowy rainbow images are my only waking suspicion of non-recollected dreams. What to do now?

It's late afternoon. I don't see anyone I know outside. A fickle breeze is pecking at the palm leaves that drape the garden. I've heard that the Maharishi Mahesh Yogi's Transcendental Meditation Center is somewhere down the river and outside of town. Spending a solitary day surrounded by strangers involved in unsettling situations has left my nerves uneasy. I'd like some familiar company, but . . . since no one's around, I decide to hike to the TM Center on my own. Grabbing my journal, I set off again.

I never get there.

The walkway is crowded and noisy thanks to squads of kids running in the sand and setting off large firecrackers. Small groups of them gather, set the match, *scatter*, and a few moments later, the explosive burst—*BANG!*—kicks up a ton of sand and unleashes their delighted giggles so they can run around and do it all over again.

I'm feeling duty-bound, though, and pressed to get to my destination and return before dark, so I don't pay much attention to anyone . . . until the shyster's eyes steal mine and his smile promises more than I'm desiring.

My flesh turns bumpy, and, for a second longer than I want, I'm locked in his visual embrace. "Who-Ever-He-Is" looks about twenty years old with a dashing teen screen idol beauty that would easily sell fan magazines in the States. He's leaning against a water fountain exuding a cocky invitation that reminds me of one a deadly spider might offer the fly she's trapped between her teeth. I keep walking, tossing an automatic smile his way, which I immediately regret. I'm shook and I know it, but I can't figure out what about him haunts me. Why do I feel so uncomfortable? An eerie, repulsive sense of possession wraps me in shivers.

I keep putting one foot in front of the other, keeping my focus on forward momentum and setting a racing pace that's tiring me.

It's just been a long day, I decide, and that shyster lad is probably just a residue of unresolved fears and anxieties left over from my earlier meeting with the teenagers. I chuckle at my foolishness.

"Onto the Maharishi's," I promise myself, feeling, finally, like the captain of my own ship.

The last building along my route before the town's sidewalk ends is set along a squat, two-story, red and yellow ashram whose sole distinguishing characteristic is its colors. I've heard it's the one ashram in town that purposely caters to long-term stays of Westerners. It's said to have a full schedule of classes teaching various yoga disciplines, meditation, nutritional practices, prayers, et al. Approaching the end of this structure's property, I can see up ahead where the pavement ends and the dirt foot path heads along a wily S-curve into the thickly shadowed, forested corridor.

I'm being followed!

My blood crusts into icicles. No new sounds alert me, but my ears are scanning for any distinctive footfall or breathing. Some part of me knows it though and is broadcasting a warning in Surround-Sound®.

I'm being followed!

I'm six steps short of the dirt path.

Step.

Should I do the woods?

Step.

It's dark in there.

Step.

"Bail out!"

I slow and step to the right of the pavement and sit on the rock wall that partitions the path from the sand. As I kick my legs over the other side and settle myself, I open my notebook, then turn my head to see who's been following me.

Damn! It's the shyster. There are a few people on the walkway slowing him . . . no . . . he seems to be limping. My throat closes tight as if noosed. I feel the path beckoning to the left. The beach stretches wide before me and I want to run, yet I feel that, run as I might, there'll be no escaping this guy. I've got to face him.

"Who the devil is he?" my psyche screams, and, even while doing so, I keep telling myself it's okay, not to worry, there's some purpose in our meeting and a couple minute's conversation will sort it all out. I'm just tired, that's all . . . I hope!

"Hello," he says, having surreptitiously circled around to my side. I turn. He has no sense of personal space or is choosing to not allow me any. Only inches separate him from me. My smile returns his greeting but doesn't loiter. I deftly return my attention back to the notebook on my lap.

"Hello," he repeats.

"You speak English?" I ask him, shifting my leg in order to turn and look more directly at him.

"Ahhhh," he exclaims, and pulls my notebook right out of my hands!

"Hey!" I grab for it, but he pulls it back, places it down on the wall, and begins turning pages.

My breathing halts for ten seconds, but I pull back my hand, recalling the boys on the sand and their innocence and the fine time they'd had. I hope this will turn out to be the same.

He speaks while continuing to turn pages. I think he is asking where I am staying and, for some unfathomable reason, I tell him.

"Parmarth Niketan."

In turn, he points at this red and yellow structure whose name I cannot make out and tells me that he is staying there. After a second's hesitation, he tells me he will be in Parmarth too.

Gloom descends over me.

"How much to stay there?" he asks me.

I decide I should shut my mouth and tell him, "I don't know. Someone else is paying for me."

"Is it there nice?"

I nod and wonder what he's leading up to. I want to relax, but I'm too afraid.

He talks more, but I can't understand. I shake my head. He nods and says it again, but nothing is comprehensible. Is he really speaking a language I can't understand or is my mind refusing to let me hear what he's saying? Which came first—the fear or the feared? More and more, I fear this isn't going to be like all the other peaceful encounters I've enjoyed in India.

His eyes dance and dazzle and play wizard-like games in my mind. I can't look at them anymore! He is still saying something that is indecipherable, pulls a paper from his vast shawl and. . . . Oh, no! As he spreads it out before me, in that second, I see his huge malformed foot—full five times the size of a healthy one, and I know what the well-worn paper says and shake my head and hands "no," grab my book back, and pull myself away.

I'm not falling for this letter, don't want to touch it or be anywhere near this man with the dangerous eyes and Elephantiasis. It doesn't matter that my learned mind is correcting me that there's nothing really wrong with him; there's no contagion; he's perfectly healthy. Something about this *man* is not healthy, and I don't want anything to do with him.

"You give me money."

In novel-esk fashion, my jaw drops from shock.

"No," I answer, laughing, disbelieving his brazen manner.

"Yes, you give me money," he answers, his words now clearly understandable.

"No," I answer firmly.

"Yes, you will give me money for me to stay at Parmarth Niketan. You *will* do this."

He shows no doubt, just smiles that sly, sure grin of his, and I'm getting angry—which is a sure sign I'm scared or hurting. I *know* I'm scared. What I can't understand is the gnawing sense of hurt that's becoming more and more real. I don't know what this old hurt is. Perhaps centuries old, in the cycle of reincarnation.

"Listen," I tell him, rising from the wall to stand full height beside him. "I'm sorry you have this illness, but I am not giving you any money, and you are not going to stay at Parmarth at my invitation."

My little speech only broadens his grin and emboldens him.

"You will give money, or I tell Swami you have promised this to me, and now you steal this back like cruel joke. I *will* stay there. Or I will wait for you every day in the entry until you give me money."

Shit! Am I going to end up spending the remainder of my idyllic-till-now stay in Rishikesh either trapped in my room avoiding this man or being stalked by him every minute?

"*NO!* Go away! Leave me alone," I yell, anger finally raised in defense.

Still, some counselor in my head keeps urging me not to become involved in this melodrama, don't play the *game* or be infected by his thought. Keep still, impartial.

I draw a deep breath and use all my might.

"You will not get away from me," he says.

Panic's boiling me alive!

"Forget it, forget him," urges my inner counselor, but all I want to do is strike this man, scream, knock him down and run far, far away. My counselor keeps talking to me—"Forget it, Forget him"—even as my imagination plays out revenge-filled fantasies as repulsive to my spirit as they are comforting right now.

When you fight a war with yourself, the only one likely to get hurt is you, and so it is that my rage does its damage. In moments, I'm too bruised and haggard and numbed to even feel angry anymore.

"Have a good day," I finally tell him. I heave a sigh that weighs a ton, and I step over the wall. He remains standing silent while I make my way across the wide expanse of sand towards the Ganga. Recalling his threat, I decide to follow the river back towards the more populated town. I weave through the first stretch of boulders laid upon the beach thick as measles spread across flesh. I figure the young man's bum leg won't allow him to circuit this terrain.

A few minutes stroll north, I stop at the water's edge and relax to hear its song. It's speeding by and I can almost hum its chord. Its soothing presence brings peace enough again to me that I crouch down at the shoreline and pray for greater insight and understanding into all that is happening this long day. Just thinking about how angry I'd been rings tears from my eyes that seem never to end.

I try to ferret out what is causing all this to take place, but I can't. I hadn't acted like me back there. Matter of fact, I don't recognize any bit of who I'd just been. Even back home I don't draw such people or events to me, but there seems to be some kind of barricade preventing me from understanding this that I can't climb over or walk around or break through. It's got a protective device wrapped around my psyche refusing admittance, refusing investigation.

Then images of the youth's strikingly beautiful facial features coalesce in my mind. I wonder how long he has had this disease and how it must have affected his life; how his family, how his friends reacted to the growth as it began taking over his appendage, and how their reactions created restrictions within him.

Is the threat I felt radiating from him a product only of my imagination? No. No! Absolutely not, I argue. He made his desire too plain.

What does it feel like to live off live prey?

For this boy to intrude upon others, using the malformation of his flesh to stir the fears of others and have them empty their wallets just to be free of him—to use his condition as a weapon as pointed as a knife to steal from others . . . would his own rage and pain from the "trick" fate had played on him make the transition to such a life easy? Or had he been a shyster of sorts prior and had merely adjusted to another scam?

Scam? How can I even *think* that? Do I *really* believe that? He's made a choice of how to get by. For him, it must seem like the best option available. I can't conceive of how I'd ever survive such a thing. Then again, in the spiralling corridors of times and life-hoods, I probably have survived—or not—that and worse. But this boy has certainly stuck something right in my face to think about. What is it about him that's stoking my fears?

I close my eyes to the beauty of the river, the hills, the beach, and the sky to find an answer. I feel like a blind woman must walking through a room filled with fragile, antique mirrors.

Yet, something bleeds through membranes of my masked awareness, and, suddenly, I begin praying for this beautiful boy; this boy whose life has been disfigured, whose mortal plans for this life have been so dramatically altered. May he know his own beauty and strength and lead a fulfilling, satisfying life. May his presence humble those who aren't, and open hearts to question the reason for pain so that each of us begins acting in ways that eliminate pain from ours and the lives of those whose paths we cross.

I've been standing here for awhile. Eerie shadows are falling across the late afternoon sky. My eyes leave the horizon for a second to rest on the dampened sand around me. That's the first time I notice the moon at my feet.

My hand grasps the full weight of a rounded, silver-gray rock. Yes, no doubt about it. Clearly impregnated in charcoal tone on its surface is the design of a quarter moon. It's magical to be holding the moon in your hand. I drench it beneath the Ganga's water to cleanse and energize it. The moon is not washed away, and I'm thrilled at the feel of its solid presence in my palm. Silence passes, disguised as time.

Several very grateful moments later, still deep in thought, I stand and prepare to leave.

"Hello."

I turn like a top and am immediately entwined by those sly eyes and clinging smile.

"I follow. I told you."

"Just leave me alone," I order him, my newly birthed compassion completely eradicated (I'm a perfect person only in my meditations).

"No," he says and adds a laugh to taunt me. "You give me money."

"Go away." My voice is hard as concrete.

"I follow. No escape."

What a cocksure son of a. . . .

My frustration is burning a big hole inside me. What can I do? His coal-black eyes are laughing. He is mocking me. There really is nowhere to run. My anger delights him. Fear feeds him. What a mess!

But it's his life that's messed up, not mine, I remind myself. I may not like what this guy's doing; he may be a frustrating pain in the butt, but I sure can't hate him. If he's not going to stop doing what he's doing, *I* can at least choose to act differently.

"Listen," I start, lowering my voice and stepping closer until our noses are less that a foot apart and my own stare so deeply into his he can't help but look away. "What you're doing to me right now is not going to help you. It just makes me angry. What you're doing makes it harder for people to care about who you are and what you need. You've been hurt, so now you want to hurt. Something's been stolen from you, and now you want to steal things. That doesn't make things better. That just keeps everyone defensive and angry."

"I wait at Parmarth everyday," he promises.

I've done all I can. I take off across the sand, stepping easily across the tops of the multiple boulders blocking my path. I don't bother looking back. He doesn't have to follow me now that he knows where I'm staying. I know he will be looking for me there.

"God, I am *really* confused," I cry to a dusky sky that seems acutely void of any answers. I stop looking for answers, blanking my mind somehow and keeping the direction of my steps ashram-bound. So focused is my intent, I'm not physically aware of where I'm walking, barely registering my proximity to the town's walkways, and not noticing, except on later recall, the sudden yelp of running children fleeing my path.

Uncharacteristically, I trip, hop, side-step quick left and grapple for balance. It's some other woman—surely not me—who is walking and hears the deafening BOOM and sees the flashing orange explosion inches from her raised right ankle. The flesh-and-blood-me doesn't even slow my pace. It's the children running towards me, their eyes wide and fearful, who shake me back to awareness of where I'm standing and how close I've just come to maiming my leg.

The smell of gunpowder fills my nose and lungs.

I nod to the children, quickly reassuring them "okay, okay" until their faces light up again, and they run off to set another firecracker.

Meanwhile, I'm rooted in place after they leave, my eyes shifting the sands around where I'd just walked, following the path of my indented steps and finding the burnt, tattered remnants of the explosive.

"There are no accidents," my inner counselor advises, and I know that my misstep was no coincidence. The who that I am and the choices made in my life have just combined with other forces and spared me the round of potential trials such a life-altering "accident" would offer. So . . . I can learn from the explosion without necessarily experiencing it? Just like I can learn from the boy? From my own self-inquiry? The process of the experience doesn't have to be physically endured or suffered.

It's all too much. I can't, don't want to think or allow myself to feel anymore today. Later in the evening though, lying in bed, still shaken by the all-engulfing day I've experienced, I pray for no dreams, pray for no thought, and dive deep as a submarine into sleep.

I sleep through the speaker-amplified morning chants for the first time. My roommate is already gone by the time I rise. When I step outside at 7:00 though, as promised, the shyster awaits me on the path. I spot him first. He's sitting comfortably on one of the benches bordering the garden walk. My heart sinks but my feet don't. They rebound me around the corner and down another lane leading me towards town where I can merge with a crowd of touring Indian families who are just departing through the gates.

Despite my escape, his presence troubles me. As I walk towards the post office, I worry about him popping out of nowhere to hassle me sometime during the day, but my coffee vendor spots me first, calls out in Hindi, and points me towards the balcony where several of my friends are already gathered. Their happier stories and adventures envelop me. The shyster is washed clean away by their laughter and the sound of the diamond-backed river that's being licked into whitecaps this morning by a ripping wind. My day passes happily and without a single thought about that boy.

Today, several days have passed, and it is a new morning, and the boy and I see each other for the last time. I'm standing outside the swami's quarters sharing stories with two men from the kitchen staff when the shyster walks by accompanied by one of the regular ashram staffers. Their heads are bowed in serious conversation, but sight of me paints the conniving gleam and wide smile back on the lad's face. Only, this time no noose strangles me. This time there's no tie left between us. I'm even relieved to find he's found someone who may be able to help him, and so I greet the shyster with a smile before returning my attention to the two men who so kindly have been serving and cleaning up after our meals.

There is still so much I haven't fully, consciously understood about this one day's interactions. I've awakened from sound, seemingly dreamless sleeps with one or all of these fellows the first thought on my mind. Often and inexplicably, discomforting images of a leper's foot, inquiring boys, or the shyster's grin will flicker across my thoughts—my prayer, my plea, and the unforgiving sense of self out of all time that helped bring us to the day's resolution still seeks greater illumination than my conscious mind will accept and abide.

Frustrations. . . .

I keep expecting some thunderbolt of wisdom to shake me to my knees with a vision of our complete meaning and purpose to each other. No thunderbolts, no visions come, but some shifting has obviously occurred. So, perhaps, as the explosion exemplified, the rest doesn't matter.

CONVERSATIONS ON THE SANDS OF TIME

"On the Ganges one year, a century, or even a thousand years was much as another; the only difference was in the seasons— and here on the sands in the middle of it they were only indicated by the level of the water and the power of the sun and the rain."
—Eric Newby from *Slowly Down the Ganges*

"Are you sick, Miss? They have medicines in the town."

I draw a deep breath and hold it, continuing to sit scrunched up like a ball with my head stuck between my knees. I wait; I pray for the man with the kind voice to go away. I don't want to raise my head and expose my tears to even the sun's glare, much less some foreign stranger's gaze, while on the banks of the Ganga.

He hovers still, and it's obvious my Western programming of stoic silence will not appease the innocence of this Eastern man's genuine concern. I shake my bowed head "no," even as still another lunging sob breaks free.

"Damn! Who is this guy and how do I get rid of him?" my silent scream implores. I wipe away the flood of tears rampaging over the dam of my silence. I just want to be alone! I want to cry in peace and get it out and over with! It's not working out that way.

"You have fever?" inquires the sweet voice.

Oh, God, to be a foreigner in a foreign land! Maybe he'll back off if I expose my tears. Surely there's some sort of protocol about that. I uncurl and bare my reddened and streaked face up towards his shadowed figure.

The deepest, brownest, quietest eyes I've ever seen touch mine. I've never seen this man before but something about him seems oddly familiar and calming, and I know in this moment that this dark-skinned Indian will not be leaving soon; though, what we will talk of, or why, I've no idea.

"You sick?" he asks again.

Yes, I am sick, but there is no bottled cure for it. The river is my poultice, and toxins are pulled and flooding free of me with every sob and tear—toxins of fear, frustration, anger, doubt, confusion are shed freely upon the sands.

I've been fulfilling a promise to myself during this trip and allowing great amounts of time for introspection. This morning I'd retraced my steps to this favored writing place, settling myself in a remote spot just shy of the tide pools. All I could do was gaze into the cloud-free, sapphire sky feeling some vague inkling that there was something . . . *something* I was supposed to know or feel or remember.

The sun ignited everything in sight. Even the river rocks jutting up from the driven water blinked like signal mirrors. Then I saw something, no, *sensed* something more real than sight or feeling, something *beyond* the walls of the town or pine-laced hills, *beyond* the sky, beyond even the light of day. I'd strained my eyes, raking the very air for the substance that pulsed and swirled beyond my senses, and eventually the fibrous gatekeepers guarding the inner me opened to some informational energy flood that bombarded me like pulsars. It was like an explosive birthing of some luminous star releasing from me!

Emotion . . . emotions . . . memories beyond mere memory escaped in the salt of each tear. Emotion of ages gone by; old, old memories eluding distinction as pictures or events, recalled only as texture and sensation seeping from beneath the earth of my flesh and running as a great tide reflecting in the Ganga; memories of lifetimes when the river flowed, the ground was tilled, seeds planted; lifetimes when orders were hailed from man to man, when soldiers marched and saints prayed; memories of meditations on these banks and multiple foreign hillsides, and cycles of living, playing, working, and dying; of priests and kings and knights and great floating vessels; of agreements pledged eternally; even the promises made in this lifetime as a child—and broken as an adult—to never settle and to always live better. All of these pooled and swirled awake.

How far afield have I wandered, and where, oh where, might be the path back?

My entire existence seemed drawn from me like juice from fruit. The weight of all my past decisions that have not been for the highest good rise and fall from me, released into the vat of the great Ganga, but I've floundered in these images too long and can't escape. I'm sucked deep into the cesspool of those problems I've so recently released. Like a tire parked in mud, spinning my wheels only digs me deeper, and I can't get out.

"What can I do?" I'd protested, knowing instinctively that without some kind of plan, without the nourishment of a healthy thought, without an inoculation of *some kind* of support, this emotional debris will only fester and grow plentiful again.

Exhausted and desperate, I'd finally exhaled "God, help me" to the square of sand and chunks of stones I could see gathered around my feet. In response, on top of everything else, this man shows up and asks if I'm sick!

Yes, I am sick! I'm frustrated, angry, confused and doubtful all over again, too! But . . . this is nothing to speak about to a stranger. Instead, I construct a smile on my face and point to the roaring river.

"No, I am not sick," I tell him. Touching my hand to my heart, I add, "This is very holy ground."

Something in what I've said or how I've said it impresses him. He straightens his stooped posture. I think he will leave at last. Instead, he gathers his cloak about him and gracefully settles himself down besides me. His walking stick, made from a course tree limb, and the small bucket pilgrims carry to gather their food hand-outs in, are laid to rest beside him.

He is utterly still from inside out. I watch him with equal measures of caution and curiosity. A chorus of dire childhood instructions warn me not to speak with strangers, but my curiosity about this man with the kind voice and gentle ways who, for some inexplicable reason I sense some deep kinship with, shoves those long ingrained fears aside.

At first, I thought he must be old. Now I see he is not aged, and unlike other pilgrims and beggars I have seen, this man is not gaunt, though his brown, full, round face has been sun-dried and his lips are brittle. He exposes yellowed-teeth stained a thick brown in spots. I expect to be repulsed by his body odor or some other smell from his travels, but there's not a whiff of anything unpleasant despite his close proximity. His well-used robe is basically clean, and that relieves a certain residue of wariness.

He sighs and rubs his short-cropped, unbrushed hair in a habitual slow motion. Every motion he makes is slow, I notice. His eyes seem to rest on everything at once without moving and examine the inside of everything; not like those crazy guys with that wild-eyed, conniving "I've got your number" sort of look whom I've passed on streets in New York or Los Angeles. There is nothing deranged or intrusive in this man's manner. The spirit of this stranger who's sitting beside me breathes a peaceful, reflective, inquisitive pace.

I scan the area around this desolate beach of boulders. Where we are sitting is far from, but fronts, a long line of "shorefront" Rishikesh ashrams that line the sacred Ganga River. Despite the flow of foot traffic on the far-off, dung-dappled cement, the two of us are, miraculously, alone. That seems uncanny. I recall how, only minutes before, I'd implored God's help.

"Is this guy some kind of angel?" I wonder.

It's an odd thought for me. I've only recently begun entertaining those kinds of ideas. Maybe that's all it takes to let them come wandering into your life when you're down and out and feeling rotten and needing a hand—belief and a prayer? My curiosity about this cloth-draped man is piqued.

We begin speaking slowly, his mumbled statements prodding me, and shortly after the conversation begins, I realize this is no poor peasant or beggar as I'd first imagined. He speaks thoughtfully phrased English, hesitating often to find the right translation for some simple question he has. He inquires on a multitude of subjects and holds some political opinions. That adds up to a degree of wealth and education and, I hazard to guess, probably a career (if he isn't an angel, that is) when he isn't wandering along the Ganga speaking with tearful American women.

"I have had fever, but am released from hospital," he tells me.

Fever? I hate disease and tense immediately. In the last few weeks, Dengue Fever has killed hundreds of people in Delhi, though it hadn't apparently spread as far to the north of India yet as we are sitting. It's spread by mosquitoes, but is it contagious between people, too? As if to reassure me, he adds, "I have note from doctor I am well."

Considering all the other unpleasant notes I'd been tricked into reading, I'm reassured by the fact that he doesn't offer it to me.

I nod and wait to find out what we are here to talk about.

Across The Miles

"From where do you come?" he finally asks.

"America," I answer, feeling just now more akin here than to that seemingly foreign continent of my birth.

His sweet smile graces me. "You . . . like this land? India?"

I nod, again touching a hand to my heart in what seems to be an instinctive motion not ever used before this day.

"What of it appeals?" he wants to know.

I take a deep breath and look at the brisk, quick river for a long time, listening to its omnipotent roar that calls great things out from the depths of me.

"India is the soul of this world," I answer. "The people here, in their devotion, in their simple worship, in their quiet faith, belief, daily prayers, and offerings to God and to this great river that nourishes and cleanses them—I feel these people hold a reminder in place for the rest of the world's people who have forgotten about God and love and the essence of life."

A quick sparkle in the corner of his eyes signals his surprise.

"What is America like?" he wants to know, and the instant thought of America's size, variety, and the sweep and spectrum of its concerns overwhelms me. How to distill a succinct description of it for him?

"Big," I finally answer, laughing a hearty laugh which finally catapults me free from my mucky mood. I feel light again for the first time in a long while.

He grins a shy grin because, I'm sure, India, too, is big and vast and grand, covering millions of square miles of mountains and plains and marsh. Every region of the country is different from every other. Homes, religions, landscape, commerce, clothes, handicrafts, etiquette—even the materials and quality of the prayer beads gracing the necks of the more than 930 million inhabitants vary from region to region. India has always beguiled and challenged visitors, even to this day.

It is a land of great wealth and great poverty; of political concerns and corruption, and also of unflagging idealism and activism; a country now where spiritualism and materialism vie for acceptance and balance; where the new attempts to negate the old, and the old clings still and efforts to shape the new; where aged structures line streets bordered and traveled by modern structures and mechanics; where disease is fought with modern medicines and cured with ancient elixirs and faith; where death is accepted as integral to life; where adults and children laugh, cry, play, love, work, wonder, and die so they can live again.

So, how is it I would dare consider America any different or greater than India? It's just a perspective, the singular one I'd been taught so very long ago. Listening to this river flowing nearby, I play with the grains of warm sand sifting through my fingers as my mind replays other conversations I've had upon the sands of the Ganga during this journey to India. Feeling the peace of this man beside me and my own attunement to this place, I sense a cohesion, a connection that's escaped me before. Oneness? Are we really more the same than we've previously imagined?

"What are the people in America like?" he inquires, raising his head and displaying a broad, impish grin and thick, brown-encrusted teeth. "Is everyone rich?"

Ah, America, the Land of Opportunities. There have been evenings I've sat watching television in my Pacific Northwest home when I'd cynically considered those opportunities mere myth. No longer.

Yet, I don't feel it is wealth or the dream of wealth that inspires this man's question. To those living half a globe away, America is like a fairy tale, a land of aspirations, possessions, possibilities, and ideals passed along from one person to another in tales and verbal repetitions of newspaper articles, and its story sparks the imagination and stokes the fire of dreams. I wonder about this man's dreams, but decide to wait a moment before asking.

I tell him, yes, there is great wealth—and great poverty—and many, many people with comfortable amounts of money and uncomfortable amounts of worry in-between those extremes. Those with financial wealth sometimes own more worry than those living financially impoverished.

He listens as I describe big cities and smaller towns I've lived in or traveled through, the farmlands and the corporations. Quiet and seemingly unmoved, he thoughtfully studies the sand lying before him while his chapped hands stroke and pat the short, dusty kernels of hair upon his head. Slowly, slowly, continually stroking, listening, he takes everything in with more than merely his eyes and his ears.

How much of this he's heard before from others I don't know, but it seems as if he's hearing this for the first time, or like one who has no reason to doubt or to question but only to hear the answer to what he's asked.

I, too, am listening to my answers, and I feel as if I'm experiencing America for the first time, accepting and understanding a greater aspect of the people born within its borders and, as well, of its own destiny as a country.

"You do not mention, uh, land . . .," he struggles to describe something, "land . . . like this," he tells me. His gentle, doe-like eyes inquire of mine.

I don't know what he means and shake my head. His arms raise to embrace the whole vista.

"Are there places like this, holy ground, in America?"

Like this? I'm about to say "no," but instead close my eyes and seek something I believe I'm being called to see beyond the physical.

The silent thunder of the powerful Himalayan range breathes behind me, merging with the roaring song of the Ganga that's coursing through me. Rishikesh, long held to be one of India's most sacred cities, translates as "City of the Divine." It is in the heavily populated north country, but it still remains a relatively isolated town, a difficult, rutted, and dusty six hour taxi drive from New Delhi; or a three hour train ride can transport you to the closest major city of Hardwar where, again, a cab can be hired for the final 15 mile trip to Rishikesh. People travel here because it is "holy ground."

A pulse, like the heartbeat of the earth, moves inside me, and a light show of fluttering memories unwind. There is, I see, indigenous wisdom and spiritual consequence on all the earth. Now I feel the Sacred Ground hills of Pryor Mountain on the Crow Reserve I walked in Montana. I hear the raging waters of Oregon's Breitenbush River along the banks of the retreat center where, for many thousands of years, native peoples would travel hundreds of miles for healing in the sacred pools. I imagine the ceremonies of those Native Americans who have come and gathered for generations at power places like Devil's Tower in Wyoming. These are revered for their energies and the message bestowed by beings of other realms to the peoples who've honored Spirit for so long, but the mass of the American populace doesn't recognize such places.

"Yes," I tell my patient, nameless friend, "there is holy ground in America, though I don't know all there may be. It is not like here where pilgrims have travelled for thousands of years to worship at certain cities, or live or pray in the mountain caves, or how some have built the ashrams so that the many more can gain greater understanding of God and life and be filled themselves with that sense of wholeness and unity with God."

What more, I wonder, can I tell this quiet man of my personal perspective of America without having it, incorrectly, appear a harsh place. I see it more as a diamond in the rough.

"Most of the people I know in America do not yet know or necessarily seek spiritual Oneness," I continue, careful always to speak slowly and allow him to understand and absorb my meaning. "They have not actively sought wisdom as is *still* done here, despite Western influence upon India. In America, people busy themselves with jobs, earning money, and buying things to gain some temporary satisfaction or pleasure."

In India, religion is inextricably intertwined with every aspect of life. The people live close to the earth, frequently sleeping under the stars, journeying to the rivers and mountain shrines to pray. They see the stars and experience nature more than most of us.

I tell him that every city and town has many churches or temples or gathering places where people of differing beliefs may attend services and worship in their own way. As I share this, though, I remember opening the Seattle Yellow Pages and counting approximately 2,100 churches representing 122 overall religions/means of worship. That discovery had troubled me at the time, because Buddha, after all, sat beneath a tree; Jesus spoke on hillsides, in town squares and along the waterways; Zoroaster, around fires under the stars, in caves, and upon mountains. All the masters had stressed natural connections with the Universal Force. Yet those phone directory listings demonstrated how people have created a plethora of specific pathways to God and secured our beliefs behind denominational walls.

Unlike India, whose inhabitants will make pilgrimages to holy places at various times to purify their bodies and spirits, I tell him most people in America don't know or yet understand about such places, and those that do usually end up traveling instead to sacred sites of other countries. Many magazines advertise spiritual journeys to the pyramids in Egypt or Machu Pichu, the Holy Lands and the Western Wall, "or even the holy lands of India," I laugh, aware of where I am standing.

"Things are changing and the time will come soon," I add, "when people everywhere will understand that all the earth is sacred, how energies affect us, and that we *too* are sacred. What do you think?" I ask.

He seems surprised that I ask him.

"Yes," he begins with hesitation, "earth is sacred. Energy. Hmm . . . energy. This energy all around. Many people do not feel it though. No, no. They *feel* it, but they do not *know* it. You know?"

I'm not sure and shake my head again. He searches his English vocabulary for the words that might explain.

"Some people treat other people good. Yes? They smile and are nice, help. Helpful. Other people do not treat others good. Sometimes with words, and sometimes what they do, and, or maybe *not* do, from what they *feel*. It . . . touches me."

64

I'm nodding, and he is suddenly grinning and nodding, this uncharacteristic animation demonstrating pleasure in my comprehension of what he's struggling to communicate.

"The town," he mumbles, pointing towards Rishikesh, "no good. . . . Used to be people more peaceful; people would pray. Be good. No more. People now talk about God, but they do not live what they say. No heart. When you stop feelings of the heart, you *shoot* at me," he insists, raising his arms as if aiming a rifle.

I'm stunned. Words, deeds, feelings, whether spoken or unspoken, can heal or wound, maim, kill—as lethally as a gun. This simple man has expressed a powerful truism. I grab my journal, telling him I need to write this down.

Now he is confused and delighted. "What? Why?"

I tell him because it is so very true what he's said and so beautifully spoken. He smiles and laughs and laughs, watching me. He giggles and shifts his place upon the sand, moving his hand again, as usual, round and round over his scruffy skull. I am enjoying myself also, and it's because this man has warmed my heart.

Spirits On The River

Moments pass. I wonder how old he really is. Either his younger eyes have spied a recent spiritual decay in the town, or this man is older than the wind and his insight harkens to past eras of mass spiritual devotion.

"This town no good to cry in," he adds, recalling my sensitivity. "Good here," he says, pointing to our wide-open sanctuary of sky, sun, and sand.

I think I know what he means, and it is more than just the physical separation of sitting in private on the outskirts of the main drag. It has been hard for me to sense, much less release my fear, renounce doubt, and ask God for help surrounded by sturdy structures that help keep those feelings in place. There is nothing to fall upon, to cradle me, warm me, or comfort my spirit. Cement seems so dense, walls so confining, crowds so erratic. It is hard amidst such energy to know how much of this coldness, racket, and nervous energy I've felt is really mine, versus the crowd's, and to discern my own warmth and clarity.

When seeking clarity back home, I've always gone hiking along the mountain trails bordering my home. Yet, in Rishikesh it is the banks of the Ganga that call. Its voice lulls me to sleep and soothes my predawn Puja waking, always shimmering inside me, always moving within my mind.

This river seems to run through me, magnetizing every cell of my body. It calls to me, and something from the depths of me responds. At various times of the day and night, I find my steps turning towards it, finding new places to sit and be still with it for hours on end.

I ask my new friend about this. A tiny smile spreads like a slow leak across his face. He pulls his robe up around him in an artful manner that allows him to squat. It's a common and easy pose my knees have not yet adjusted to. Here, people are born without the thought or need of chairs that seem not only uncomfortable but an unnecessary luxury.

"Through all time this is as it is," he explains. "Ganga cares for all of us. Ganga feeds. Ganga washes, nourishes, cleans. You pray. Offer yourself to it. Give doubt, give pains, give troubles. Talk to Ganga of all you have been foolish, all the hurt you have caused or feel. Bring it to the river. It will take. Ganga knows."

The people have done so for centuries, he tells me. Whether they are performing worship, ablutions, exercise, bathing; whether drinking, chanting, praying or being, finally, set ablaze on its banks after physically dying—the Ganga is life to those who feel its flow and honor it.

"Leave worry. There is no reason," he says. Indeed I see none upon his face, nothing troubling the vistas within this man's eyes. "Let go to the water and live your life free. It is better."

He looks to me to acknowledge that I understand.

Something like volcanic lava percolates deep within the crust of my body's own earth. What kind of instinct is this that's drawn me like a hound following a scent to experience joy and contentment, to release emotions I'd not known even existed, and to feel so quiet and peaceful next to the Ganga's banks? Have my daily pilgrimages to these waters been prodded only by memories I hold from past lives lived along it? And, if so, in all the memories and emotions that I've released to set sail upon these waters in recent days, have my recent realizations freed my soul's past aspects from their karmic burdens? Freed them and brought greater illumination, strength, and alignment to my soul and to my divine life?

How ironic that a complete stranger brings this lesson home for me. It is something I have been taught, but it had not been commonly taught. This tranquil man beside me feels like a hovering spirit, and, suddenly, the image of us two being spirits on the sand stirs my imagination. It feels like I'm talking to myself, or rather to some part of myself I'd not yet met until today, or like some aspect of myself I'd once been.

Hold it! Is this *me*? Could this be *me*? Pilgrim or beggar? A wandering seeker? A disciple of some specific religion? A solo being seeking only the solace of sun and stars? Maybe all the above . . . many times? Have I drawn more to me than merely a lesson but also a personal messenger? And what might such a re-introduction mean?

He is picking at the frayed ends of his cloak's left sleeve, oblivious to the long lull of space and time we share. I wonder, in the moments between our conversations, does his mind catapult like mine to other ideas, places, and galaxies? Or does he merely take in what is and lets it be.

Suddenly, though, he asks me about *the medicines*. "Do you have cure for cancer? AIDS?"

Why would he think that? Ah, yes, of course, I marvel. In the mythology, it is America who could do such things, after all, if any nation could!

I laugh, tell him "no." I tell him we have many chemical medicines to make people feel better, but that I don't believe they truly cure. He laughs like a child when I tell him how doctors are now realizing some of their medicines and chemicals create illness, but they believe the odds are worth continuing dispensing of the medicines because they don't hurt enough people for it to be considered serious. He is almost giddy when I tell him people die because doctors quote them statistics proving they probably will die—so, of course, more people die on cue, and the percentage that proves that "fact" continues to rise in growing proportion.

"Yes, yes, it will," he chuckles, rocking back and forth. He knows, he says, "the energy transmits," and we agree doctors who believe they have all the answers are silly; and we agree people need to know themselves better. Then we talk about what is natural in healing.

In India, there is extensive use of Ayurvedic and herbal remedies. They are sold in pharmaceutical stalls throughout towns, and at least one ashram has a naturopathic/Ayurvedic clinic on its premises along with a regular hospital. In India, food, too, has been considered as sacred as the human body, and, despite the onslaught of Westernization, there is still an understanding by many of the necessity of eating foods free of chemicals.

My friend mumbles to me that the medicines of the doctors in the towns are too expensive, that the doctors of such great training in the universities no longer know how people want to be well and do not hear what the people tell them of their troubles. As usual, he inquires of America, and the quantity and diversity of our medical doctors impresses him. He appears unmoved that our treatments are also expensive, and he's amused that American society does not yet believe herbs and other such treatments are acceptable and effective.

"That is . . . silly?" he chuckles, grasping for the American verbiage. "They must change their thinking?"

We begin to talk of the power that the human mind has to create and to heal things. I am not sure that he and I are "tracking" each other completely anymore. It is difficult to understand him. His words begin to fall from his mouth as if clumped in honey. Most times, too, his head is bowed or he's paused to gaze at some distant sight where his mind seems also to journey for gaps of time. His muttered responses to some of my inquiries don't seem to match my questions. It's a confusing few moments, and I suspect some part of his religious background defines things differently than I'm able to grasp. I am many words behind him in translation and utterly confused.

Doffing my confusion for an idle minute, I muse over what the doctors may have told him about his fever and how he had reacted, but I'm too late in asking about it, because, like a loosed puppy in a shoe-filled closet, his interest has strayed onto another object. He voices unflattering opinions about the Indian government.

"The government here, India, no good. They are not running our country well. They are thieves and liars! People are not treated good."

Such harsh assessments startle me given the gentleness and still-ness of this man up to now. However, during the several weeks I've lived here, I've learned many have their own reasons to be unhappy or amused by the government(s); everyone has a bone to pick, it seems.

One day a man whose home I was visiting asked his little boy to sketch pictures for me. The man was proud of his eight year old artist son who would "one day be a priest," the Brahmin[12] father informed me through a translator. The first picture the boy drew for me was Mickey Mouse. Everyone gathering around chuckled in praise of the child's talents. The second sketch, however, was a simple lampoon of the country's local leaders which earned the youngster guffaws and a hearty slap on the back. How easily beliefs—and animosities—can be transferred and reinforced. It had been an insightful experience in many ways as I pondered what attitudes I might reinforce in others through statements I might make.

These musings are interrupted by my friend who sits reposed like a monkey in the sand, perfectly comfortable with himself, holding an elbow balanced on his bent knee and the flat of his hand settled upon his head.

"America is great country. Correct?" he asks, displaying a delighted whimsy on every feature. I think he may have been wanting to ask this question from the first, and my other answers about America have not deterred him.

Now it's my turn to laugh at the myth and wisdom of perceptual prisms that disguise our similarities as difference. I have no knowledge of India's policies and governmental structure, nor of the in-depth un-derpinnings of our U.S. government. I am a single person as is he, as are we all. However, I know there are greater truths than the singular viewpoints expressed by individuals.

---

12   In the Indian caste system, Brahmins are the highest class and, traditionally, hold the place of priests and the intellectual class.

"Well," I note, quoting his earlier statement, "there are people in America who would say that America is run by thieves and liars."

Horror contorts his face. "Really?" he gasps.

My laugh relaxes him and his worry is replaced by an appealing curiosity.

"It is degrees," I tell him. "Levels of awareness, you see?" I ask, doubtful that he does just yet. "I believe there is great movement in the spirit of people. Institutions and those who run the institutions don't feel this spirit in the same way because they are so bound inside the walls of their beliefs and policies and self-interest. Self interest, you know?"

He nods and I continue.

"And those of us who are outside the walls, like you and I, can see much further, feel and experience things differently because we are free of those walls. I think we are fortunate because we are the ones who believe in something finer and are free to plant new ideas, do things differently and create change."

He is weighing this, nodding, digesting what I've said, which is a greatly appreciated personal reward for the effort I am making.

I ask him, "Don't you think it is funny that the land you have come to hold as 'perfect' in so many ways—America, I mean—is charged by some of her citizens with the same problems you voice of India? It is people, evolution. That is all. It will change as *we* all change the way in which we treat others."

His frown is now wrinkling the whole of his tender face. "But . . . are not all Americans rich? All have what they need?" Obviously my earlier explanations to him about wealth and poverty had either not been understood or not believed.

I like the open innocence of this man and the gleaming wells of his eyes. Gazing into the depth of those eyes, shudders again run through my body, loosening knots long curled inside me, and I'm grasping a greater awareness of probable purpose(s) in coming together.

In the past of many life-hoods, surely I have wondered about the haves and have-nots, about injustice, about when there will be a balancing of accounts; and surely in all this world there are people seeking wiser answers than their fears and doubts and accusations would attest. Surely in the centuries of my journeys upon this earth, I have been a holy one and a sinner, an official and a scoundrel, rich and poor, friendless and sick, prosperous and healthy, wise and not. So, in the telling of our stories and asking of our questions, perhaps he and I are bridging divisions between former selves and new selves, between our cultures, and our beliefs of how things have been and how things can be. We are each like drops of this clear expansive river we have returned to. Within each of us is the whole of the river. My heart is touching his and his mine.

Or . . . is he really an angel, after all? Perhaps, because I certainly have no fear of him, nor do I hold judgment about what he chooses to do with his life. An educated man who chooses to take up a pilgrim's bowl? Something tells me this journey is a choice for him, and it is our mutual choices that have brought us together along this deserted patch of boulders, rocks, and sand. The peacefulness, the quietude, the give and the take, the acceptance, the mirth are all healing.

He waits for my answer.

"In many places and for most people, it is quite good," I respond. "Not like here where so many have so little." My mind recalls the tenuous construction of huts and homes, men lying on wood beds set out on the dirt, insistent children begging and poking their hands at me.

"In America, there are good homes, food, and many things to buy, but for many it is not so; particularly for the Native peoples of the continent, there is great, great poverty. Everywhere in the world, the poor are still poor no matter how much everyone else may have. So, I believe America is close to finding the answer, but hasn't quite grasped it yet.

"Some people," I add, "believe America is not as good as even I tell you, and another person may tell you it is indeed a perfect place. The truth, I'm sure, is beyond anything any one mortal might say."

He grins. As a Hindu he has been raised to appreciate the expansiveness of God's vision versus the limitations of our mortal viewpoint.

"But America very important," he insists. "I think, I think America must come and *take over* India."

My jaw drops, and he talks quickly despite my shock.

"Yes, yes. America has great know-how. America get things done. India too slow in some things, too old."

Again, his conviction gives away his breeding.

"But what would you want America to do?" I ask, confused about his request.

"America must run country, manage factories. America has machines and tools to do work fast, faster. Easier for people. Labor hurt. America will make things better for us."

I let a long pause rest between us.

Weeks ago, I'd been in New Delhi and visited the site where Mahatma Gandhi had been shot. Two friends and I spent a long time watching the people walk to the grassy knoll and the simple marker. Singly, as families, and in couples they came in reverence, in curiosity, and in sadness. We wondered what the passing of such a man meant to these people. In Gandhi's endeavors was a call to the spirit of the people to feel their own greatness, their own divinity, and not let outside influences control their own. It seemed, as my friends and I watched the people, that their movement and their prayers were acknowledging Gandhi for what he'd done and all he hadn't the time to do. Gandhi, I think, would want them to know it is *them* who must do.

Now this man sitting beside me is saying there are those who still seek another to do it for them. With all the wisdom this man has demonstrated today, with all his sensitivities and his caring for the people and the land, I cannot understand how he could feel this way.

"Do you really think someone else, an outsider, can make things better? Isn't it better for the change to occur within the country, for the people to decide and choose and create their own change?" I ask, intent on understanding.

He admits there are others who do not agree with him. "They say that if that happen, the outsiders would just treat the people bad. They try tell me it has been done before many times by many countries who have robbed us, but I say how much worse can it be?"

Business, the government, and the environment must be improved, he asserts. If his government can't do it, and, he says, is actually preventing it—then one that knows other ways must.

I feel utter sadness for the first time since meeting this man. I have been a distant witness only to some of the lack and poverty in this land

and its people. Yet, I've also felt and seen the riches in the gems of their eyes, the music of their laughter, the aroma of their warmth, and the crystal clarity of their spirit.

"It is odd to me that you say that," I respond gently. I don't want to insult this man. "Earlier you told me how terrible it was that the towns and cities were losing their essence, their holiness—and the people, their reverence. Remember?"

He nods.

"You told me, 'People now talk more of God and spirituality, but they do not live it, do not live what they say.'"

He nods again, and I continue.

"Well, the West, and America, has forgotten much of its spirit and is having to begin anew. The country was founded by men of great belief and faith and idealism, yet in a very short historical time it has come about that self interest, greed, and efficiency—*not* compassion, kindness, faith, and love—are the forces that create policies, create commerce and corporate decisions, create even our favorite games and enjoyments. Many people who attend religious services do not see the sacred in all life and do not live their divinity towards even their own neighbors.

"So," I continue, "no, I do not understand why you would want America, or anyone else, to *take over* your country. Yes, your people might be driven and profit by the knowledge and tools of the West, yet they might also be brought to greater depths of poverty or lose their desire to know God, as has already happened in the West. This is the very thing you say you most regret seeing even now happen here as influences of tourism and business arrive."

Words and movement are silent between us for many, many minutes. A slight shifting catches the corner of my view, and I shade the strong sun with my hand. Scrolls of gray smoke are rising restlessly skyward on the far reaches of the opposite bank. Cremation or just trash disposal? It's too distant to make out.

My friend has finished his silent musings about what I've spoken and clears his throat. "It . . . it is not something that has come before to me," he tells me. "Can think more on it?"

I nod. He's certainly given me enough to think about today.

My notebook catches his eye now, and he points and asks what it is.

"It is my notes," I answer. "I am a writer."

"You write what?"

"Whatever is important to me," I say.

"Ah," he intones, then reaches for the wirebound pad and opens it. I grasp for it, but he turns my hand aside tenderly. "Why do you write?"

I notice the pages are being turned with care. To another person, I might have said, "It's just my journal to remind me about this trip." But I'm beginning to sense this pad is more than just that, and instead I say, "It is a book about this sacred river and about the holiness of the earth and its people, how they touch me and are like me and everyone else in every way, and how we can all experience that."

A nod and another "ah" is his only response while his fingers move like a butterfly across the sheets, opening each page so it can fall and allow another to open. Pages and pages scrawled thick with blue ink open and fall, intriguing him like a toy entrances a child.

"Give me pen," he urges. "I will write address."

I hadn't even considered the possibility that he could write, or that he'd even assume I wanted his address.

When he's finished, he passes the notebook back to me. The address is in Cut-tack, and his well-defined handwriting announces he is to be addressed as "Mr." The beauty of the penmanship is another verification of a higher level education.

I try to thank him, but his mind, eyes, and fingers are all pointed at me.

"You must go to Nepal. It spiritual there. Feels good. People live good."

So, is this some kind of clue? If he is an angel, might this be some hint about an experience I need to have that is of great personal meaning for me? Unfortunately, the logic and financial limitations of my planned itinerary shove such considerations and angelic instructions aside. Maybe next trip.

Meanwhile, his hands are ferreting the notebook from me again, and he writes the name of a "tourist place, understand?" (a hotel?) and a couple temples that "are good." His penmanship is as profoundly slow as his thought and speech are careful.

"You or your family have money? Family rich?" I ask, feeling like an intrusive foreigner.

"Yes," he hesitates. "Family rich."

He tells me he is in agriculture. I'm not sure what such a phrase means in India. Is he a farmer, a landowner, or does he work in some business having to do with farming? Instead of asking, though, my focus turns instead to listening because his words are slurred again, and I can't make out many of the disjointed translations. I think he is saying he will begin his return to his family the next day. Where and how far is Cuttack from here, I wonder. Why has he come? Why would a wealthy man of business (wealthy being a relative phrase in India) be dressed in such a cloak and wander through the towns?

I could ask, but I'm afraid of prying, of appearing like a pushy American while the Indians are such a gentle people. Perhaps this is his way of worshipping God. Perhaps it is like a many-week's fast from mortal needs, where he renounces the "food" of life's comforts and business garments, of a warm kitchen's nourishment, of friends and family's familiarity, of worldly acceptance. I think that perhaps in his belief, and I don't know if his personal beliefs might vary from his ingrained Hindu beliefs, standing so singular and separate is a way to find God, to know truth, to feel life.

And then, inside my gut, I'm crying, "I know this, I've done this," and what a revelation to come face to face with the place I've evolved from and to feel the evolution of my soul's knowing!

I have seen the pilgrims and beggars and the sadhus sleeping, strolling, and sitting along the creviced roads and walkways, and I'd assumed, at first, they were just statistics of India's financial poverty. Yet, now some short's been rewired in my head, and I realize these people are living their devotion, faith, and love of God in their way. It is now, and has been for millenniums, right and good and necessary for the many more of us to experience God as the God within another person who may shuffle past us on pilgrimage. It is an exchange, and it's personally profound and humbling to understand that my soul has grown from the nourishment of such a devotion into my present day belief that, while one does need to make homage, one does not have to sacrifice a life in order to live a good one; that God loves the purity of the "saint" and "sinner" and is waiting the day everyone accepts the riches of our abundant world; that in the silence of our Being beats the pulse of God.

This man is both student and teacher to the soul he is and the souls of others whose paths have and will intersect his. I am fond of this brother who has found his way to me.

To Live

"What is your vision of the future?" I ask him, certain that one who treads and speaks so softly is hardly likely to espouse Armageddon.

Indeed, he tells me that he believes, "It will be a good world . . . beautiful world."

His eyes have taken on an other-worldly hue. "First, though, there will be confusion and angers and wars—like now—but then people will understand and change to peace."

He believes peace is 70 to 80 years out. I tell him a decade or less which surprises him, but we are at least heading in the same positive direction. The ultimate intention of our thoughts is what will lead us all to the intended destination anyway.

"What is it you dream?" I ask.

He doesn't understand. He looks at me calm and wide-eyed, curious for me to explain about "dream."

"When you think of the future, *your* future, what do *you* want?"

His muted laughter discards my query lightly. "Nothing," he answers.

"Nothing?" Now it's I who doesn't understand. Surely dreams are the elixir of civilization.

"You dream of nothing?" I sputter.

"In sleep, pictures come, but this is not what you speak of, correct? Dream?"

"Correct."

"No, nothing," he states. "I do not dream for something. You want, what, your car? New house? That is not what makes you happy. I want to *live*."

His spiritual sincerity speaks of a life beyond a dull existence. He is, he's already told me, of the Hindu faith which, I know, holds everyone to be born into castes. I know that the four main castes are divided up further into thousands of sub-castes that function more like industrial guilds. Opportunities for jobs, education, travel, family connections and marriage, earnings, socialization, acceptance are prescribed by castes. While the government officially outlaws prejudice based upon such considerations, the people's daily lifestyle nourishes it. So, I wonder, how would dreams enter into such a life?

On reflection, though, I hear conversations with my neighbors who each have their own definitions of what living is all about. On "bad days" some have groaned about how hard it is for them to "go on existing like this." I wish they could sit where I am now, not so that they can compare their wants and pains with others and thereby judge themselves more or less fortunate; but, that they would learn to experience the beauty of life as this man and others do. India is a land where people who have nothing share everything with you.

"You give me tissue. I will wipe my nose," my companion says very precisely.

A simple need I can easily satisfy. He uses it instead to dab his eyes for many moments.

"Is the caste system here good for people?" I ask.

Perhaps other Westerners have argued with him about it, or perhaps it is such an established existence in life as to not deserve questioning, or perhaps he thinks I understand more about it than I do, or perhaps. . . . Well, at any rate, my friend offers me little response. I listen carefully to hear him tell me in a monotone voice that it "is good sometimes, like for work. Other times, not."

I wait patiently for him to offer more to this answer, but nothing more comes.

Two thirsts have been existing inside of me this day. One, the spiritual, is continually quenched, but my physical needs are not. After sitting beneath the molten furnace of the sun these hours, my flesh and throat are raw, the skin of my face bronzed. The gurgle and sparkle of the flowing Ganga has been teasing a thirst that's now become a desperate yearning for liquid refreshment. My imagination is brimming over with the taste and images of cool sodas, even as this man's presence reminds me I can satisfy this desire easily because I have the money to afford it. I wonder what, if any, food is carried inside the deep pockets of his robes and within his silver bucket this day? Part of me wants to continue shifting through the sands of time together, to continue our simple talk, and another is pleading and urging me away.

I tell him I must go.

"Yes," is all he says as he tilts his head and stares at me guileless. I'm surprised . . . and hurt. He is free of desire for more, accepting what we have given and shared, and he's willing to release us again to the paths we choose. He seems to live in the silence between thoughts.

Not me. I don't want to go, yet my throat is screaming for water, for cola, for anything wet and sweet. My eyes are pulled to the sparkling river that I've watched so many drink from. I'm considering it. Two days earlier, a gray-haired Hindu man, who'd watched me praying on the water's edge one sunrise, had urged me to drink. He'd hurried over saying, "You are very, very lucky," and bent down to dip his tin cup in the waters. "You are here. Drink the waters. Drink only Ganga water. Not town water. Drink only this water. Be healthy. So lucky, you." Then he'd hurried away.

The Ganga runs wild and cool only a few feet away from me, and my eyes ravish it, so wanting a sip. On another day, an Indian naturopath had told me how safe the waters truly are. She said that Westerners believe the waters of India are contaminated and they are sickened by it, yet, she argued, "But you have it opposite; the wrong way. You have so chemicalized *your* water, chemicalized *your* food that all that is *natural* in the foods and the stream now sicken you. Your body should be able to accept this. Our bodies do. Westerners who have kept clean the irrigation systems of their own bodies do. They drink and it is fine. Your sickness is your body telling you to cleanse, and so it vomits or you have diarrhea. That is how the body is ridding itself of what are the truly foreign particles trapped inside your bodies."

It had made sense to me at the time. It sounds so inviting now . . . but I still can't touch my lips to this water. Bottled soda will do, I decide.

I rise to go and ask if he wants another tissue. I don't know what else to offer him.

"No." A simple response. His last. It's delivered without so much as a parting glance.

He really does not seem to care I'm leaving. I, on the other hand, feel like one magnet being pried from another. My feet drag as I plod up the sand, finally reaching the crowd-thronged walkway. Colorful booths beckon me, and I have to step carefully to avoid people, laboring horses, cows, and the blankets of vendors that are spread across the way.

The very reality of this man plagues me. What will he do? Where will he go? Perhaps I should have offered him food or a soda? I stop and look back to the piles of rocks where we'd sat. He isn't there.

"What the . . .!"

I stop in my tracks and a swarm of people weave around me. My eyes scan the sand and river scenery. I can't see him. He's nowhere.

Is this some kind of twilight zone where material and spiritual dimensions overlap? Confusion and thirteen different possible explanations dance jigs across my mind. I look left, right, center, down, up, around. Where is he?

Did he leave? Is he behind me? I turn, but he's not following me. So, where is he? What kind of magic is this?

I turn back to look at the boulders and . . . now he's there, his muslin-draped back turned to me. I can almost feel the quiet stillness of him as he sits there actually living his desire "to live" in every moment. Slow motion, he is lifting something in his right hand from his lap to his mouth while looking out over the waters. What does he see, I wonder? What does he think?

At first, I try to imagine this man who seems to be both young and old holding any job, and I can't. He seems part of something beyond the activity of daily physical life. His destiny seems to be the act of sitting upon the earth, and he is sitting exactly as he should. Yet, if his job really is in agriculture, he is very well placed. His stillness speaks of his respect and faith in the spirit thriving beneath the flesh of the earth.

I'm tempted and almost run back, wanting to talk more and study those illusive, lingering movements of his; the motions which move without movement. I'm tempted to explore more enigmatic fragrances of past remembrances released, but my thirst is biting sharp as agitated wasps, and I know I've got to move on.

Thanks to this man, the future I'm stepping into is now filled with a montage of multi-colored dreams. I'd always thought I had dreamed before. I had goals and things I wanted to do, and I listened as people advised me to make them real by visualizing them, and I thought I had been. Now I know better. It dawns on me that I have not even begun dreaming before this moment, and that I am even more like this man than I'd felt. Like him, I have placed screens around the circumference of my imaginings. He wants to live and so do I, and our lives reflect all we've thus far dared to imagine life would allow. I have not yet allowed my soul and my imagination to soar as high as they truly desire.

He and I leave reflections of one another upon each other that will sift through the sands of time, and I wonder how our present selves will begin to reflect future selves that will be affected by today's meeting upon this river of reflections.

I see him still sitting there and whisper my thanks and good wishes for this man's well-being, and cast one final gaze over this spellbound setting to hold it fast in the net of my memory forever.

CLEANSING EXPOSURE

*". . . Join the ranks of the celestials who are pleased with you.
Illusions have ended. Let the fever of your heart be dispelled. Here
is the celestial river, sacred and sanctifying the three worlds. It is
called the celestial Ganga. Plunging into it, you will attain your
proper place."*
—the *Mahabharata*

Patience was born here. It is a pattern. It is a pattern that allows time to not exist, or at least, to pass unnoticed. It fills the lungs with something other than oxygen so that breathing is not necessary because breathing takes time. It empties the mind of pre-patterned imagery of pasts and futures that create time born of other places. It births corpuscles of singular moments. I can sit here forever and yet be here only now.

The pattern of life here is much like the man I am watching on the rock.

He is squatting on a large, irregularly rounded river rock less than three feet across that is jutting up out of the powerful waters. This is a fast running section of the river, and even the water's edge is pulled by the tide. I've a sense of how fast and wild it can be further out because on some days I've sat here and witnessed river-rafting crafts shoot rapids at breakneck speed and spout an occasional tourist up and out and into the drink. Yes, there are businesses in Rishikesh that cater even to the spirit of adventure!

I'd thought some overpowering need to pray had driven this brown-skinned man to roll up his pants leg, step into the water, and slowly, if unsteadily, make his way out to the rock. Now I see he is doing his laundry. The wad he'd been grasping in his hand is now unveiled to be a sheer white shirt, while the other hand holds a block of some sort.

He is the sole presence on the outcropping and secures his bared feet at an angle I wouldn't have trusted, his every action focused upon what he is doing. Squatting, he dangles the shirt down and drenches it in the tumbling water. The shirt is lifted, drenched, lifted again, and finally splattered flat on a small section of the course rock between his feet. With the care and attention a carpenter might give an intricate carving, this man sets himself to the task of washing. The block I'd seen is obviously some type of laundry soap because he's scrubbing it deliberately onto a section of the saturated shirt he's spread open.

He scrubs and rubs. Another section the same. Next. Again. Again.

Now the shirt is beaten against the stone again and again. Clumped together, it's mounded like bread dough, pounded and pounded and mounded again to be pounded again and again, then rinsed again in the water, flayed in the air and onto the rock, beaten over and over again against the rock. The man's every movement is rhythmic, seemingly effortless, focused upon each individual act, requiring no movement additional to the well-chiseled chore his arms and hands are set upon.

This task is completed, and the still damp but cleaned shirt is left in a roll beside him. Still squatting, he pulls off the white shirt he is wearing revealing the string wrapped around his body that designates him a Brahman. I am surprised. I've assumed that caste also designated the degree of wealth one might have and that no one with any money would be pounding their shirts clean against river rock. My assumptions are obviously wrong.

This shirt, too, he drenches in the churning water, scrubbing soap into the material, and the cleansing process begins again. He never looks up, but keeps his eyes to the task. Watching him exposed so singularly upon a rock in the midst of the river, I begin thinking how close to the elements all these people live.

Everywhere here, you are exposed to nature. The shops are open-air stalls. Many people, by choice or condition, sleep outside. Homes most usually consist of only a single room and are constructed of simple mud or clay brick; their entry "door" may be only a plastic sheet which cannot insulate their inhabitants from the earth and natural forces. The odors and sounds of cattle, multiple peoples, the mountain chill, stagnate street puddles, flowers, manure, floral-scented breezes, running water, urine, horses, citrus, vegetables, hillside meadows, curry, clouds of scuffed dirt co-mingle over the entire area in a sensory stew.

It is outside, beneath the sky's canopy, where people meet and talk and debate, bathe, cook, play, launder, pray, barber, and shop. They are not all prey yet to the limitations imposed by modern innovations; their movement and attention are not wired by either telephones or television to the confines of buildings. The river holds their prayer of thought and feeds them; the river, the wind, the sun, the rain also nourish and cleanse body and spirit of the people as well as the earth.

Before my departure for India, people complained to me about all the poverty I would see here and wondered why I would want to go. For a short time I, also, had worried about how I would react. Now I know that impoverishment is a myth. I don't mean people aren't poor, and I'm not romanticizing the very real hunger and illness and suffering experienced by multitudes of people spread over the 1.27 million square acres that is India; nor the pains of all the other world's people. But watching this man stooped upon the rock starts me thinking about focus and attention, creation, and the passage of time.

I project myself, figuratively, beside him so that I might feel more about him and understand why he's doing what he's doing. Imagining myself upon the rock, I balance and bend to my laundry as the chords of this river continuously flow around and beyond me, and the cords of my muscles and flesh of my back and legs stoop and stretch to my task of washing beneath the blazing sun. I feel perfectly secure, my feet well-placed on the solar-warmed rock. I don't wobble. I don't worry. Something non-physical buoys me. Perhaps it is the ion vibration rising from the river; or, perhaps, I feel stronger because I am standing someplace where nothing exists for me to cling to.

As I wash, I know that washing my shirt is something that needs doing. I *know* it. It is as simple as that. Hygiene is important and cleaning needs to be done.

The land-based part of me that sits watching this man from the shore recalls that, these many days, I have witnessed men and women bathing and barbering as well as praying all along the river. It is simply what they do. In the doing of it, something is renewed, refreshed. Yet, this man who has stepped into my sight this day has chosen to perch himself upon this rock. Even as my imaginary self balances beside him, I am unsure why.

What meaning can this have for me? *Of course* clothes must be cleaned. *Of course* washing must be done. Perhaps that is the point? His attention is focused on what needs doing? In the doing and paying attention to what needs doing, places and things other than this stable stone and cleanliness of the shirt are of no concern. Until the clothes are clean, those other things do not matter, are not as important?

I see that the second shirt is cleaned, and the squatting man has let his hands fall across his knees while looking up to explore the pale blue sky that's filling with bursts of powder puff clouds. Part of me is still joined with him; I have no idea how long we have been stooped and scrubbing, but I feel satisfaction in the job and, now, also feel good just sitting here as he is. As him, I look shoreward and wonder briefly who that foreign woman in the bright yellow shirt and aqua pants sitting on the sand might be and what it is she is doing. Then, as him, I sit and think nothing at all.

I leave that imaginary me resting beside him, return my attention for the moment to my station on the sand, silently slipping again within the reality of my yellow shirt and aqua pants, and allow my mind to wander another pathway.

The people of India are a patient folk. Foreigners who can't read the shaded lamps of their eyes might interpret them as resigned or reserved, but the Indian eyes I've looked within reveal long-secreted treasures they themselves have sometimes even forgotten they possess. How and why is this? What have they mastered that is so hard for the Western mind to grapple? Then the man pops back into view, and I wonder what *is* patience anyway?

When I'd projected myself onto the rock beside him, I'd felt focused. And, yes, patient . . . peaceful even. How odd! I've always believed focus to be a blind-to-all-else, efforted concentration that gets you something or somewhere. Now, though, I'm thinking that maybe it really doesn't have to be anything other than rapture in the moment of being. Maybe it is my belief that chooses to either effort or enjoy each concentrated moment, each thing I am doing? If I focus my intent directly upon the needs or desires of each moment, does it expand that minutia into all that is in even *less* time and eliminate worry of what was before, comes later, and the why? And does that create a "later" *earlier* than might have occurred otherwise? If so, patience that is filled with such peace as I have been sensing in this man is born of strong belief, not resignation; acceptance rather than worry; caring for needs rather than needless cares.

Perhaps impoverishment dissipates when we live in, as, this state of rapture?

Yet, what would distract from doing what needs doing, I wonder, and what needs doing? From this man's perspective, good hygiene is important and needs doing. What else? This is an easy answer for me—filling everyone's belly and allowing everyone to be as free and great as they are able to express. Could living in such a state of moment to moment attentive rapture bring this about?

Perhaps a patience of such peace is born here because it is where spirit thrives? Here is where the monkey god, snake god, cow god, mountain god, the rain and sky and river and sun gods, and gods upon gods continue to be celebrated and honored. I haven't been able to keep up with the *Who's Who* of deities in residence, and it is just as well because the pillars of this primarily Hindu land also throb with the life force of Buddhism, Jainism, Sikhism, Sufism, Zoroastrianism, Islam, Christianity, as well as the other varied indigenous animism worship and more secretive Tantrika.

Oddly enough, as oft-conquered as India has been over the centuries by multiple nations sweeping down upon it from all directions, none have been able to rob the people's faith, nor the gems from their eyes. The wealth of India's spices, finery of their cloth, and the rich jewels buried beneath the earth were all the invaders sought, not realizing what lay hidden in plain sight. Apparently spiritual faith, then as now, is highly prized only after it's been tasted.

It's a marvel to consider how often some European or Latin American nations have been raided and the spirit of their people demolished or intrinsically altered in some way. The essence of India's people, though rocked by Capitalism's fever, maintains its poise on the rock of their faith.

It seems to me that India's soul is like the rock this man I'm watching is standing on. Its soul is set in the river, because this river is the heaven-sent elixir that continuously refreshes the soul of us all.

Is it, perhaps, fortuitous that, by and large, the people here are linked by lifestyle to nature, entwined with the cycles of seasons, and continually fed by the elements and the river? Do the songs of these forces continually re-attune or hone the people, however subtly, to fundamentals that distractions deafen others to?

It would be easier, given the comfort and convenient lifestyle to which I've become adjusted, to judge this way of life inferior. It is harder to admit that all my culture has and strives to attain, for all the good these things may do, actually lack some fundamental ingredients that make our treasure-trove pale in comparison to the riches held by these people; that our culture also lacks key elements which might turn us from the promotion of false needs. Do we really need to manufacture 100 different varieties of facial blush and screwdrivers of the same color and size when there's a child starving somewhere?

It is harder to admit that in creating a perpetual hunger to own the biggest and the best of the most "things" we can, we actually create poverty in the lives of others as well as within ourselves. How hard it is to admit that we live forever judging others and ourselves when we could focus on our rapture and create satisfaction for all. It's no longer impossible for me to imagine everyone having *at least* what they need.

Are these people really impoverished? Perhaps that is more than perception? Perhaps it's also transient? Holy man, Yogananda, in his classic book, *Autobiography of a Yogi*, described the millenniums of India's material prosperity and its many contributions to the world. He then described the poverty so evident during India's last couple hundred years as ". . . a passing karmic phase." India's patience is apparently pacing its way through this cleansing also.

In light of that, I wonder now what karma might the beliefs, attitudes, creations, and actions of my country be empowering. And, comes the shuddering question, what creations are *my own beliefs* focused on?

Before I can answer that, the man on the rock has risen, re-rolled his trailing pant legs, picked up his shirts to shake them open like sails on the breeze. Now he's stepping gingerly into the discombobulating current and rocky-bottomed riverbed that slows his progress until his pained feet finally touch dry land. Here, he slips on sandals I hadn't noticed he'd left on the shore earlier and walks away at a quick pace.

I turn back to stare at the rock that's held him. It seems now more like an empty stage. The dazzling dance of lights jiggling off the water surrounding it mesmerize me, and I wonder more about the coincidence of that rock and this man and the choices he's made. Shifting slightly in my seat, I watch his figure disappear into the distance, and I'm again stunned to realize how far off the beaten track he'd walked in order to situate himself on a boulder so close to me in order to scrub two shirts clean.

He'd cleaned what needed to be cleaned, stepping away from all else, all distractions, all other beliefs to stand attentively upon the rock. I'm grateful to him for allowing me to experience his focus and to also discover that balance and focus are instinctive and peace the result when we choose to stand upon the intent of our soul.

MURAL

"The Ganga has been a symbol of India's age-long culture and civilization, ever-changing, ever-flowing, and yet ever the same Ganga. She reminds me of the snow-covered peaks and the deep valleys of the Himalayas which I have loved so much, and the rich and vast plains below where my life and work have been cast."
—Jawaharlal Nehru, first Prime Minister of India.

Visitors entering the courtyard leading to the private office of Swami Chidanand Saraswati ("Muniji") at the Parmarth Niketan Ashram in Rishikesh are now greeted by the sight of the rushing, green-blue and white-capped waters of the Ganga charging down its snow-laden Himalayan mountain staircase and through the spring-time greenery of pink and yellow flower-dappled meadows far below.

During our visit, some of the silent visitors who've waited in the foyer for entry into Swami's meeting room have been able to witness this colorful mural birth and spread itself over the breath of Swami's garden wall. Their smiles and wonder-filled expressions translate their foreign whispered words into those of universal understanding.

Perhaps no less amazing than the scenery suddenly curtaining this place have been the handful of casually attired and paint-draped American women and men, of whom I am one, freely walking in and out of this courtyard. We stand and balance precariously on tables, file cabinets, chairs, and other furnishings that have been stacked to act as

88

a type of scaffolding, one rickety piece on top of the other on top of the other. We come and go as we like, each for our individual reasons, volunteering various quantities of time to help artist and international muralist, Sharon Walker, channel the flow of the Ganga to earth in her artistic way, much as it's believed Shiva allowed the sacred waters to flow through his matted hair from heaven to the Himalayas.

Several times a day, Swami passes through, his movements so still and smooth and vibrant, he appears to float above the grass.

"Isn't it *wonderful* the love, the *love*! Across the oceans we didn't know each other and now, here, we are sharing so beautifully. This is *beautiful*. Such a true gift of love," the bearded holy man gleefully tells us whenever he passes by.

He is a world leader of Hindus and a busy man with multiple responsibilities called in from all around the globe, and yet he loves this mural being offered him, and he makes time to consider it and our effort meritorious of his attention. His enthusiasm is boundless, cradling tides of ideas, wisdom, and joy. Our brushes, thick with green, white, brown, blue, or pink paint always stop traveling across the speck of creation placed in our charges long enough to enjoy his enchantment with the changing vista he sees.

Through his acceptance of this gift and through the good and happy energies we share and intermix, a new bridge is being created that will somehow help others cross the gulf of divisions that have separated people from each other and create heaven in daily life. Such is the potency of giving freely.

This mural is a two-week labor of love. Its progress is sometimes diverted by human tributaries of illness, long meditations contemplating what and how to paint next, forgetfulness, lack of paint, spills, the need to attend ceremonial events, plain exhaustion, or a desire to simply relax, shop, and enjoy the town for a few hours. Yet, despite our interruptions, this mural is living up to the holy river's heritage and continues thriving in the flow of its destiny TO BE.

To me, this mural bridges the strong twin beauties of fore and aft. Lying parallel before the actual physical presence of this and other ashrams, homes, and shops runs the holy Ganga River. Behind the human structures sprout the foothills of these holy Himalayan mountains. And *now*, symbolically set between these mighty energies in an ashram devoted to God and love, sprouts the effusive free range of their co-mingling currents pictured just as on the natural, uninhabited, floral earth. No buildings or people intrude within this picture. It is a raw energy of promise, strength, and free flowing joy that is eager to fulfill obligations and which pleasures in simply BEING.

This painting speaks of how life is to be lived. It is like a new born babe who is never to lose its innocence, its patience, its strength, or the expression of *its* destiny TO BE.

SEEKING HIGHER GROUND

"No man may come before the face of God, whom the angel of waters lets not pass. In very truth, all must be born again of water and of truth, for your body bathes in the river of earthly life, and your spirit bathes in the river of life everlasting. For you receive your blood from our Earthly Mother and the truth from our Heavenly Father."
—from *The Essene Gospel of Peace, Book One* translated by Edmond Bordeaux Szekely

The declarative presence of the Kailashanand and Mission Ashram shrine, its 13-story, bright, white and red turreted structure clinging to the foothills high above Rishikesh, calls and awaits the arrival of all whose spirit (and bodies) are moved to navigate the winding trail leading up to it. I'd seen it rising up out of the mountain trees, dwarfing them, on my first day, and I've noticed and wondered about it everyday since without taking a single step towards it. The magnetic pull of the river has kept me close to its shoreline.

A particle of our time today, however, is dedicated to this trek. I'm joining several friends who are also eager to climb the shrine's hundreds of steps and breathe in a sight it's likely only the local birds glimpse frequently. The views from its rooftop are said to be awe-inspiring if that is all one is seeking. For devoted Hindus, it is the intricate statues and the prayers and offerings they make at each that bring nourishment and sustenance to their lives. It is the vistas, heights, and freedom that inspire me. It will be good to again walk upon a mountain.

We are supposed to meet in the ashram courtyard in another minute. I grab my camera only to realize too late there's just one shot left. Suddenly, a sharp sound rings out. I toss the camera, grab my notebook, and fly down the stairs.

Something's wrong. Very wrong. I feel it as soon as I reach the path. What? Where? To the left.

It's a monkey. No, two monkeys. They're set on the path between my stairway and another, at the intersection that leads to and from the ashram offices in one direction and to another path which leads toward two ashram exits.

One monkey is being very insistent with the other who is hunched over and leaning against the wrought iron garden fence. Monkeys may romp along the rooftops here, but they know from long experience that their "up close and personal presence" is not desired by the human populace. They may be worshipped—or their legends are—but from afar, and they're also feared because of their long teeth and occasional attacks upon people.

This fear of the worshipped ones is not spoken of. Instead, I've seen monkeys walking along rooftops of people's homes, catching bananas occasionally tossed their way or munching on food left for them. At other times, on these same rooftops, I've witnessed the same children and adults who, before, had fed them and laughed at their antics, throw rocks at the monkeys to keep them away. The first stone I'd seen hurled at a monkey struck my own heart. The *thunk*, the shock, the dull but so deeply driven pain almost toppled me to my knees.

That human behavior had seemed so hurtful and at odds with the purported beliefs of the people. How is it that beliefs become transformed into a distant "mythology" that allows worship to reside at a place distant from our daily thoughts and actions? How can we so easily denigrate another species (or culture) to abuse? It seems a cycle played out in various ways by people in countries around the globe, regardless of their religious beliefs, financial standing, or cultural basis. Still, I'm aware it may be easy for me, a foreigner, to make such assessments, but perhaps not fair without knowing all that has cycled forward through time creating this situation. So, I've had to turn away each time I saw stones hurled from rooftops by people who claimed that space as their own.

It has not been easy to do. It feels like I've turned my other cheek seventy times seventy times. Now the monkeys are in my path, and I have to watch them.

My friends are filtering down the stairway, alert that something is transpiring. They turn inquiring looks toward me. Another woman is leaning over the third floor railing. Indians coming to and fro stop, gather momentarily, then turn to take another path around. The agitated monkey seems aware of the growing crowd and screeches and dances and darts around his buddy before his fear finally causes him to run away and desert his companion. If this one had been bullying the other, surely the second will scamper off, I think.

No. Instead, he tumbles onto his side.

My God! He's hurt!

As one, my friends and I leap forward to save him. Just as quickly, we all instinctively step back. This is not some cuddly, bedtime toy, but a wild monkey, hurt and protective of himself and untrusting of humans who, all his life, have fed him bananas with one hand and heaved stones with the other. I imagine wrapping him in blankets, carrying him to a field so he can be released and be free to heal himself or, at least, die in the comforting surroundings of the jungle that has been his home. He's doomed if he stays here! Near me, someone is urging him to squeeze between the garden fence and "rest on the earth instead of this concrete."

Whatever could have caused this? Did he fall off the roof? How could that be? Monkeys leap and tumble and rebound all the time.

What can I do? Just then, the monkey raises his face and stares up at me. That face is at once mine and his and the face of every creature I've seen upon this earth my whole life. Only, despite his pain and confusion, the face turned to me is calm, his brown eyes wide and round and alert. His jaw, though, is sliced a vivid red along one side.

"Electrocuted," I hear whispered. He must have chewed one of the roof-routed wires and electrocuted himself. Momentarily weakened, he may have fallen hard and askew onto the concrete. That would explain his broken leg.

He turns away, but that peaceful, ever so human face he'd turned towards me for just that moment pulls tears from the pit of my gut.

Why, oh why did you chew that damned wire!

He isn't old and infirm, nor young and inexperienced. He's not a solitary renegade because his companion had come down to try and help him. This wounded one has had plenty of life experience and knows the ins and outs of this place, so why did he decide to do something he'd never done before and land smack dab in the middle of where he shouldn't be? And how the heck is he going to get out of here?

I take a secondary path that circuits me around to join with my companions. Someone begins to tone. The rest of us pick it up. It's meant to soothe, communicate, heal this monkey vibrationally. I've looked into this monkey's eyes once, find them again, and lock on and hold him in my stare again for another minute, hoping he feels my desire for his health, for greater strength to leave this place, and that we mean him no harm.

More people are piling up on either side of the path. A woman friend behind me whispers to me. "Should we get a blanket and carry him out?"

I don't answer. We've all had the same idea and, luckily, we all realize how crazy it would be to try and pick him up. Those three-inch incisors can tear flesh off bone in a micro-second, and a rabies vaccination isn't available locally. She doesn't ask again. No one speaks or moves. There is just the rise and fall of tones. The world has come to a halt filled with our desire, filled with care, filled with ideas. All our unspoken ideas seem completely useless. I, we, are left only with desire and love, so that is what we use.

A minute later a guard arrives, probably alerted by one of the passersby. He steps through our gathering and strolls towards and around the monkey much like I've seen matadors strut before their bulls. He studies the monkey for a moment before beginning to shout and shake his long stick to get it to move. At first, the monkey cowers, looking back at us ("But you said . . ." he seems to plead), but then he spins and lashes out snarling, bearing his vicious, sharp incisors at the guard. I yell to the guard to back off.

He's heard me. I've embarrassed him, and the others are now also trying to calm him as well as the monkey. This could get ugly. The guard stares at us.

I feel sorry for him. This can't be the way things usually go for him. He's used to being respected and doing whatever he wants. He must feel like a matador hog-tied in place by a crowd that's rooting for the bull.

He ignores us in favor of his duty and begins again to prod the monkey away. Maybe his ego is on the line, or maybe he doesn't understand me, or maybe he won't take instruction from a woman, or . . . well, maybe this is just what he knows to do and the way things are done. What I can see from my vantage point is that, even if he gets the monkey to run, there's nowhere for it to go. The paths to its freedom are all blocked by layers of people; people who won't move quickly enough to avoid a frantic, frightened monkey.

I want to tell everyone to get out of the way. He must have a free passage. If the monkey wants to leave, let him. But I don't. Instead I listen to an admonishing inner editor who's telling me to "let them handle this."

I see the monkey. He turns now left, then right. I can feel it wanting to leave this place. I can feel his growing sense of entrapment. I feel his plea for room. I feel so badly the need to do something, but the very things I know need doing—I don't. I can't. It's like some switch has been turned off in my brain and no instructional impulses are being carried out. My mind is screaming for me to do something, to at least tell someone, anyone, nearby, that the path needs to be cleared. I don't. I can't. My voice won't come. My hand is locked around the banister.

But this guard will hurt this monkey, or someone else may get hurt. Surely someone must know what to do. The office! It's just on the other side of the path. Surely someone of authority in their accounting office here must know how to remove an injured monkey from this place!

Crazy as the idea seems, I'm at last catapulted free and run into the darkened room that's filled with people. I tell them of the injured monkey and the taunting guard. Two senior officials rise to follow me.

"Can we roll the monkey in a blanket and take it outside?" I ask as we head out the door.

The face of the man beside me curls in horror. "No, no. Do *not* touch the monkey!"

Behind these two men come the others, everyone in the office dropping their tasks to see what will happen. But these just add more people to the path, more people huddled together unsure what to do. It is a thicker, fleshier wall blockading the monkey, but at least one of the officials has stopped the guard from harassing it.

I wish the swami who heads this ashram were still here. A quick and efficient man, he'd have formulated a plan, issued orders, and actions would be carried out. But he'd left for New Delhi before dawn along with Jacqueline, the spiritual teacher with whom we've traveled. Even Samantha Khury, the interspecies communicator, left two days earlier.

The absence of these three makes this monkey's injury more auspicious. Why did he decide to chew that wire *today*? What experience is this monkey playing out for himself as well as for us? This is too public a display for any individual to claim solely. So, how do we feel? What do we see? What are we doing? What aren't we?

No one is doing anything to free this monkey, though our toning has begun again and seems to be easing his recent aggravation.

Teresa, one woman of our group, steps towards the now calmer, wounded animal. Voices of alarmed ashram officials urge her back, but she hushes them by raising one hand. I know this woman is a medical practitioner who works with many terminally ill patients, often communicating telepathically with them to learn their needs and condition—but, can she talk to a monkey?

"Be cool," I *think* towards her, hardly breathing as she slowly, steadily steps his way. Just barely four feet from the primate, she kneels down before him. Out of the corner of my eye I see a hand grab the wrist of the guard before he can interfere. This is no time for anything other than peaceful communication!

I am scared, so scared, so desperate for her, desperate for the monkey. I want this woman to be safe, this monkey to be friendly. I want this woman to tell this monkey we are his friends and want to help him. I want her to ask him what we can do. I want her to find out if he can move, where he wants to go. I want, more than anything, for this monkey to *live*! His face is my own.

They are sitting face to face, and I can almost feel, all the way over where I'm standing, the glow emanating from her. The monkey feels it too. When he sometimes turns away from her, he picks his fur or he looks skyward. Has a human ever sat like this with any of these monkeys? What does it feel like to this one?

It is many minutes before my friend rises and returns to us. I notice she hasn't backed away from the monkey, but feels comfortable enough to turn her back and walk straight over to us. We are all eager for news, but she shakes her head and confesses confusion.

"I don't know. All I get is . . . he wants to . . . go up." She flutters her hands high over her head. "He wants to go up, rise. I think he just might want to die."

"No!" I stare back at the monkey. I don't see death, don't even see anguish on his scarred, quizzical features. How can it be that he wants to die? But the sentence is cast. People are saying we need to leave and let him do what he can for himself. Others say we need to respect his desire to do what he chooses.

The others are moving, whispering, but I can't hear, can't make out anything, because I'm bursting apart, feeling torn wide open as if blasted by a grenade. Tears stream from me like blood while I desperately try to keep my insides from falling out.

I walk away, yet still see him as memories replay of all this time spent trying to save him. I know how dangerous it is for him to be confined within these walls. I know how impossible it is to physically remove him. I feel his plea for me to move the people and my own powerlessness to do so. Instead, I'd relinquished my knowledge and power to the guidance of local authorities who, in the end, seemed to know less than I and acted equally powerless.

I'm angry he's given up; hate his decision to die. I'm sorry ever to have seen him, ever to have wasted a moment on him; sorry I've given up hours of my own time, my life, for him; and, I despise these tears I'm crying for him! I could have been strolling the hills, taking photographs of temples and listening to the low gurgle of the hillside stream. Instead, I'd cared and prayed for him and all he wants to do is die!

But, I don't know about his life, or how much pain he's in, or if he can even walk, and I don't know what fate he fears awaits him here. I don't know enough about *anything* to do any good!

I take the walkway past the office that circuits around the garden and back to my building's stairway. Before heading upstairs to throw cold water on my face, I turn to look his way again. The crowds have broken up. It seems as though people are allowing him his final freedom at last. The path is clear . . . and . . . he is moving—but not far. He stops and pants hard. He's obviously pained and exhausted. I notice, off to the side, several women from our group still intent upon him. I get a crazy notion they're trying to fuel him, give him enough energy to leave. I watch.

He moves again, but collapses at the bottom of the stairway.

What will happen to this one?

He has two clear paths now. The sidewalk he's lying on is flat, but exceedingly long, and will require him to navigate a couple "L" turns and maneuver past the many people strolling through the guarded gate before finally reaching the mountain and trees. His other option is to climb straight up these three flights of stairs that will lead him nowhere but to the unsheltered rooftop. Electrocuted body, busted leg, sore muscles, discombobulated brain—it's hardly likely he'll make it. He lies on the steps for a long, long time.

I can't watch this. I've got to leave. I don't understand though. If this monkey wants to die, why is he moving, trying to escape? Is there some prescribed place monkeys go when they feel it is time for them to die? Or perhaps his will to live has kicked in again. Have we, are we, making some kind of difference after all? Maybe, but I feel useless and wasted and wounded enough. I've got to get out of here.

I spot the couple of women who were going hiking with me, but they're unsure what to do. Much of the time they'd planned for our hike has been spent with the monkey. I am beyond waiting for others to make decisions! I've got to get out of here, and I rudely offer to take one of their cameras.

"If you decide not to follow, at least you'll have photos of it."

Touching Silken Skies

I set a fast pace. My solitary march to the temple navigates a winding, dusty path, and at first I tromp along with thoughts frozen cold as ice, thinking about nothing, seeing nothing, just putting one foot in front of the other to try and get somewhere other than where I've been. Eventually it works, the seething anger of my hurt melting beneath the baking heat of the high sun, loosening with each step up the incline towards my goal.

This is hardly the idyllic ramble originally planned, but the protective cloak of my angered march eventually transforms into a paced solace. I'm still too raw to integrate everything that's occurred into a meaningful whole, but I sense the anger is part of the lesson, the releasing of it the only way to begin integration. Is it only a coincidence, I wonder, that my two roughest days in Rishikesh have been those days when I *planned* to be away from the river?

Nothing is a coincidence. Once I'd accepted that, life became more a meaningful mystery than a dull chore or unfair punishment. Sometimes, and today is one of them, meaningful mysteries are painful and confusing and not anything I want to think about. Sometimes I look back down the path to see if my friends are coming, but there's no sign of them. At one point, I turn and can see the buildings of Shangri-La and the tipi we'd raised on the grounds—along with a few dozen monkeys nestling in the trees surrounding it.

By the time I've reached the base of the massive building that's looming so very high above me, I wonder if my too-tired and shaky legs, much less my shaky interest, will carry me up the hundreds of steps hugging the exterior of its walls. I have to walk dozens just to reach the entrance. Here I must remove my shoes and officially begin my barefoot climb.

I wish I'd counted steps as soon as I began, but it's too late now. Dozens and dozens and dozens lead to the first story where people can wander along its wide rooftop and pray at the statues situated there. I feel no desire to do anything except exorcise the ill feelings I know are still stored in every muscle and membrane of my body. I take the next stairway and climb higher; higher still; still another flight. I lose count of the steps, just continue to place first one foot, then the other, upon each well-worn step of this never-ending staircase and set my sights skyward. The stairway is set so steep at one point that if it was a ladder you'd climb it with the aid of hand over hand. I vow not to stop. No one's in front of me, though I can hear others beginning the trek far below.

Something good is happening, though. The higher I climb, the better I feel. It's getting easier to relax, and my eyes sometimes leave the steep steps to glance over at the hillside beside me whose height I seem to be surpassing. My breath comes a little easier, a little deeper. I'd thought I'd end up knocking myself out. Instead, something's *been* knocked out, leaving me feeling stronger and relieved with each step up, and I forget there is any place but *here*, right *now* for me.

Still the steps rise and round up and up in front of me. The final one is anti-climactic, disconcerting, and I hover momentarily, unsure where or how to place my step. I'm left standing on one corner of a square turret that is smaller than my bathroom. A narrow walkway rounds each of the four sides, and a thin banister acts as protection.

When you look out from a higher vantage point, you can see beyond what you've seen every day, and your vision expands and starts you imagining all kinds of crazy, delightful things! In my imagination, I'm set high upon an eagle's nest looking out over what must be the whole of the world, feeling the wind rustling my coat of thick feathers as I stretch the shoulders of each wing just for the pleasure of feeling their flex. I wonder what direction I'll choose to fly off to next.

I walk around to another corner and find a garlanded and gilded statue nestled behind a protective wire cage as securely as a nest. I hardly glance at it, but I know the people I can hear climbing behind me will spend considerable time here.

Instead, I look at the scenery. The whole of Rishikesh, the rooftops along both sides of the town, specks of its beaches, the spires and domes of temples and ashrams rising out of its thick forest and hills are laid out before me like a finely set table. The sparkling river weaves through the scene as fluid as a ribbon. Beyond the buildings and hillsides that have, from ground level, blocked my views of the western landscape, I can now see the vast, and colorful green, blue, yellow expanses of this region.

It's been a long, long journey—for all, not just me—and it's not over. Yet, right now I feel free and invincible; free of the tumult and constraints and dangers below; invincible because I can touch the sky. When you feel that invincible, you begin feeling safe enough to ask yourself questions that may hurt.

The monkey returns to me. Why hadn't I insisted on a clear passage for the monkey? Why had I been struck speechless? Why had I negated what I knew and relegated it to those who knew even less? Could we really have saved the monkey? Why had I allowed myself to merely observe? Was there anything I, we, *really* could have done differently?

I wonder how the monkey's doing.

In a land where scooters are daily colliding with autos and buses, where sick and dying people are splayed out gaunt on open truck beds, where a dog lays on its side in the middle of a sidewalk panting its last breath while mobs of people stroll around it; in a land where there is not enough food or sufficient affordable medicine for the majority of the land's people—in this land, it's probable this monkey isn't a high priority to any of the locals.

But. . .I'd seen his face, looked in his eyes and felt some of his desires. The species didn't matter. He had my face, and his cheeks and wide eyes spoke to me of all the years he had spent soaring free in the trees, eating human trash, being pelted by rocks, and running and enjoying the care of his extended monkey family. Yet today, injured and cornered on a walkway, this wild creature hadn't raved or snarled (at least not until he was prodded). He merely sat, trying to figure out what he'd done, where and why he was so suddenly some place so wrong for him, gathering strength, hoping for a clear path, sitting waiting for a way to return *home*. His face spoke mortal frailty, patience, hope, and trust, even though he lacked any previous evidence that it was safe to trust. Those eyes, this being, had looked wide and innocently into mine.

There is a lot that needs changing. And there are new ways of doing these things. I wonder what might have happened if we had not gathered around this primate. Other Indians had merely passed it by. So, perhaps, we *did* some good today?

It's unlikely that people passing and observing this monkey's plight, it is unlikely the guard who was so intent on doing his duty, it is unlikely the officials who were seemingly also unsure as to what to do to save this monkey—it is unlikely many other people would have stopped and taken the time to become involved; and unlikely any of them had ever before observed or felt the things that the others and I had so obviously demonstrated for them to see.

What must they have thought! That so many Americans would, for the better part of an hour, stop their *every* activity to simply stand silent or tone to safeguard a monkey, a monkey whom those onlookers must certainly expect to die and for whom they had no particular concern, was certainly an unheard of event. That passing people would hear our low, musical, healing toning for this monkey and wonder, quizzically, curiously, "What is happening here?" and have the officials have to explain, "They are praying for the monkey. It is all right."

For these people to see, not Hanuman, their God, not a monkey of their scripture or legend, but a flesh and blood monkey being honored surely must resonate somewhere deep inside some of these people.

Perhaps part of the reason I'd been rooted in place was because I was exactly where I was supposed to be—for however long I stood there. My friends and I held a place in the courtyard that will likely grace some people's memories, no matter how confused they may be about it, for some time to come. And that is only fair and good, because these Indian people, the ones we know and the multitudes we don't, have given me, us, so much as well. Everything, everyone of us impacts others in ways subtle and unseen. Those moments register in the silence.

They make you begin to think a little gentler, act a little kinder, seek to know the greater wisdom with a clarity that, in the moment, may still be foggy; but, first you feel compelled to *know, remember, trust* that there's something good and meaningful beyond the material veil. Otherwise you just toss rocks at inconvenient monkeys who bother you; or you snarl at a loved one who suddenly is, you say, "so stupid"; or you turn your back when someone needs help. Otherwise you never learn how important it is to do what you feel is right rather than believe and accept another's authority. Lessons are experienced daily and then put to practice for the rest of our lives.

When I'm not grateful for what I see, I'm not really seeing it. When I see it, I can't be anything but grateful—no matter what, no matter how difficult it is. I saw the monkey.

How easy it is to become numbed or distracted from appreciating even the existence of things when you see them too often. Then we think we know all there is to know. We think that what we know and who we are is all that's worthwhile.

That's the pattern my life had fallen into. I'd forgotten who I was. I couldn't see who others were. And so I'd loved and lashed out; praised and then denigrated; whispered my devotion and then "forgotten" to say a simple healing word. And that's made it easy for those close to me to cycle and cycle round and round in our old habits (just as their patterns have also made it easy for me), and so we've all danced the same dance . . . until one or some of us decide to change the tune and change our ways.

There are questions needing to be answered. Alternating banana treats and stone-retorts is just another dance, a rooftop cha-cha at once both aggravating and amusing enough to prevent humans and primates involved from concentrating on anything other than the im-mediate prescribed steps, the agitations, the wants and needs, judg-ments, irritations, anger, and violence. Common, daily interactions in households around the world are often as unhealthy.

The truth of who we are has little, if anything, to do with who we are or have been, but in who we want to be, will be, and are to become. What tomorrow will bring has less to do with what we have done as it does with what we will do . . . differently. And this has everything to do with the Spirit we are who birthed us all.

An urgency shakes me. It's time to listen to the river. It is time to remember. It's time to do what we are meant to do.

Yet, my musings and I are now being jostled by a parade of people, both young and old, who've doggedly climbed the steps to worship here. The narrow parapet we share is not wide enough for two people to walk abreast, so they squeeze sideways past me, and I lean over the banister to give them extra room.

The resilience of these people astounds me, the more obviously as I watch aged men and women step past me to bow before the shrine without displaying a huff or puff of physical weakness. If their physical flesh is this strong, I can only imagine the strength of their faith. The land, the elements, the very "under-developed" nature of the country seems integral to some "higher mind's" intent of building this strength, this character.

I suddenly hear the gasps of my friends as they walk up behind me. They're happy to have finally reached the summit!

None of us speak for several minutes. They are all snapping photographs except for Teresa, the woman who'd sat with the monkey. She is looking out at the horizon. She finally breaks the silence.

"Perhaps he didn't want to die at all. Maybe he just wanted to get to the roof."

Shit! Rage . . . rage . . .*rage* flares inside me. Rage this time, not at the monkey. Rage at *her*. Rage at *me*. How could she have screwed it up? I didn't have to leave him. I could have stayed! I didn't have to get mad! I didn't have to give up!

My hands clench the banister. *I shouldn't have listened to her!*

And, I realize immediately, I didn't have to. My anger weakens to a sputter.

So, why am I acting like an ass now? I wonder. Because she may have misinterpreted the message, and now she, too, is having to come to terms with that? Would pointing to the roof have helped? Might we have done something different? Maybe. Or maybe there wasn't anything else we could do. If she hadn't at least made the attempt, we wouldn't have been any more wise. And, it was her statement that *had* caused the crowd to begin breaking up and *that* had finally allowed the monkey clear passage.

There isn't anything wrong or right in any of this, and I think it's time I give that up. That kind of judgmental baggage is what's kept me too busy, too agitated, too self-focused to see other perspectives, to understand—or try to understand—the meanings of things and how others are doing. Throwing this kind of emotional trash around has cut me off from the monkey, the others, my innermost me, and from whatever unspoken message might still have been there to be felt in the silence. Instead, I'd run away and cut myself on my own spiked fence.

Now that the anger is going away, I'm remembering everything is sacred; that there is the sacred in healing, and there is the sacred in passing. I can't even be angry anymore. I don't have to be hurt or angry, but I need to be a little wiser, a little kinder, more compassionate . . . and a little more forgiving.

Her statement has brought the others over to talk about the monkey. No one feels good about what happened. There can't possibly be a feeling worse than the sense of responsibility that you're someone's *last possible hope*, only to realize you're totally unable to do *anything*.

I let them talk, but I step to another corner of this turret, relaxing my body onto the banister and allowing my thoughts to feel the caress of the wind. Standing on the pinnacle of this skyscraper shrine, I can understand why the monkey would want to "go up." If he only made the roof, he would at least be above the tumult and on a pathway that offered some solace and a way home. And, if he didn't survive the climb to the roof, then he's ascended an even higher and heavenward staircase.

How many days, how many times during all my days, I wonder, have I allowed other things to affect me and choke my strengths, my own knowing, and blind me from seeing new things and hearing the unspoken?

It will be time for us to start heading down from this shrine soon, but I don't think I'll be returning to the ashram with the others right away. There's a little stream not far from here, down the trail a bit, and hidden behind some brush. Once there, I can tip-toe along the stream until I find a more secluded spot and just sit quietly for a little while longer.

I feel very different from before and a little surprised. It's been one thing to hear and feel the prompting of the river's roaring song when I've been sitting only yards from it. It's another feeling altogether to hover high atop a mountain and feel the river rise up, wrap itself inside me, and hear it sing on the wind within who I am.

DOWN BY THE RIVER

"Like the rain water that falls into rivers and joins the mighty ocean, all forms of gods and their worship lead to the same Ultimate Being."
—Bhagavad Gita

Dusk is a beautiful time to dine upon the river. Daylight, simmering for long hours in the cauldron of this sky, by then has thickened like a good, hearty soup broth. Stirred by the breeze and the continuous whirling of our spinning planet, vaporous blue gives way gradually to tendrils of pinks and lavenders, then grays and blue-grays that swirl through and saturate the mixture. In the latter part of the day, you can tell the meal is almost done when splashes of red, orange, yellow, and gold juices curdle across the sky and run down, transfusing the water and all else it falls upon with nourishing lusters.

The evening's six o' clock Aarti puja is food for the spirit. The aroma of its food draws me to this table, and the mingling of its aroma, taste, and my own hunger for it compel me to digest the nutrients of faith presented on this ceremonial plate.

This night I hurry to the ghat alert to the sky's brilliant citrus hue, anticipating its pigment washing into and filling the running stream of the Ganga like thick, hot oil. My bare feet slap and skid along the engraved tile of the path. To step onto the ghat, I must first pass under the high balustrade depicting the wild chariot ride of Arjuna and Krishna that continuously exhorts people to perform their spirit-bound duty.

I am.

Always, I arrive early so that I can have my own private moments, yet there are always people here before me. There is never *no one* on the ghat. The priest is just beginning to set up the altar upon which he'll lay a white cloth and set the foot-tall, bronze tree, so I know I still have time.

Before I'm anywhere near it, I always hear the river first. At its first sight, though, I gulp a long breath and sink within it, much like scuba diving, floating down rather than up, being swallowed, eased of burden, and embraced; only this time I am land-based and drowning in some sensory sea.

I look down and watch as my bare feet slip into a river that feels cold as Arctic ice. In another moment, my appendages seem warmed, but I am feeling them as if from some distant place where they are not part of a physical me I am part of anymore, and thus not something of any concern. The grand cathedral of the universe into which I've (sub) merged washes around, over, and beneath me and buoys my thoughts aloft. It is life and God I worship in silence, praying for peace and seeking to live a life of love.

The sky is darkening quickly. Though the horizon is still molten, the parting sun is winking its farewell off distant white temples. The deep silhouette of the opposite shore is clustered with bright dots from far-off windows. The pull I'm feeling of the stars and moon on the overhead stage is as powerful as the river's coursing strength against my legs. My right hand dips into the Ganga water, grasping also the reflecting celestial lights that have been flickering upon the water. One by one, I anoint my chakras with this blessed water.

When I look down again, I'm delighted to see a ship passing in the night—a tiny ship that might fit into my palm. Molded of green leaves and fitted with a tiny, lit candle, the little boat is streaming past my legs, carrying the prayers someone has placed on it down the holy river. That minuscule flame both lights the boat's way and reveals the intent of these prayers to the universal God.

It is a wide, strong, active river this little boat is set upon, yet it wobbles afloat and courses along; seemingly so frail, yet so resilient and sure, desiring only to fulfill the intent of the one who'd set it on the waters.

Actually, it doesn't even matter if it soon topples, which this one does not, nor that the little ship and its flame will likely not see much distance on this river since piles of rocks not too far downstream will likely sink it. Physical distance, longevity, is not the point. This little boat carries a prayer, and the river will swallow it whole and lift this prayer beyond the physical realm.

In the draping darkness, I can make out a few other people standing in the water who are holding little boats in their hands as delicately as they might their own hearts. One by one, they straighten their candles and light them and set them on the river's sea.

What types of prayers might these be? Anything. For peace; for the health of a sick daughter, or mother, father, or son; for spiritual realization; for greater ability to understand or withstand some pain or hardship. Prayers here are not different than elsewhere. They hold a desire for the best, never for ill. And they pray to the One God— whichever single one of the multiple Hindu Gods they may choose to name, for Hindus hold all their gods are merely manifestations of the One supreme. Their gods' lives are parables as potent as those contained within the Bible.

I sense a stir and step away from the river to join the crowd gathering close around the altar. In a space of time that's felt hours long since first arriving tonight, only minutes have actually passed. This seems one of the ways life is altered when your thoughts rise beyond the mental boundaries of physicality.

It always surprises me to turn around and suddenly become part of the hundred people, at least, who gather here each night. Tonight I see many of my friends. The women are wearing fine saris, and the men their newly purchased long shirts, and so we are mixing in with the rainbow of attire the townspeople paint. None of us are of the Hindu faith, yet we are welcome, for Hinduism doesn't restrict a person from any variety of belief. Why worship at this river? Why, too, do people here tell tales of monkey gods? A snake god? Why awaken to pray before sunrise and bother to pray again at sunset? How can such "superstition" be taken seriously? Do these rituals do any good?

You might as well ask why other cultures believe the stories of a saint's life, or why some religions pass wafers and wine as Jesus is said to have done while he'd invoked, "This is my body . . . This is my blood." There are people who doubt those events were possible!

Jostling, whispers, raised voices interrupt my reverie. What's going on? This isn't at all pre-puja behavior. What is it? The priest goes to investigate. The crowd parts. I watch him bend over the water. A smile lights his face. What is it? I'm craning to see.

Then I spot it. A snake. It's swimming and twisting in the river, flowing with the tide and using the submerged first step as its road map. Those people standing in its path had been the first to leap up and raise the alarm.

In another moment the snake travels past us and peace again reigns. The priest returns to his station where the ceremony will soon begin, but I cannot return to the same thoughts. The snake, snake medicine, is a messenger of transformation. It advises us to flow with the rhythm of life and experience willingly without resistance, to shed old skin.

The interruption serves its purpose of removing my focus from arguments.

Is it fair to judge these Eastern beliefs as "superstitious"? I see no superstition in Hinduism, only a highly refined, though human, representation of Divinity. The sublime love of Hindu worship reflects a high regard for God, for this divinity emanates from and is in everything. Feel, hear, and smell the elements, and you are experiencing God. Gaze upon plants and animals, the natural energy forces of the sun, moon, planets, and stars, and you will see and know God. These—plus art, wealth, happiness, and more—may be found in the form of a deity. It is the same with other native cultures, be it Native American, South American tribal cultures, the Celts, ad infinitum. Christian texts, as well as original translations of ancient scrolls still not widely known, quote Jesus emphasizing this essential communion between nature, man, and God. Yet, it's not the physical substances which are the point of worship, but rather their divine nature, linkage, and value to the Creator.

Just so, it is not Indian deities that my companions and I worship while we're here. It is the God of all and the One who is within me and everything else. The same One these people pray to.

I glimpse khaki out of the corner of my eye and look up to see a couple of Anglo women sitting on the highest of the ghat steps. They stick out to me, though not because of their Anglo features and the primped appearance of their skin and hair and well-ironed blouses. They stick out because they seem to believe they are separate from what's taking place. They act as though they are merely observers. They're looking down at us and the subtle preparations being made by the priest at the alter. They point at this or that and whisper and laugh to each other. Yet, no one is an outsider. I wonder how what they're observing will affect their lives. It's not as though something of this nature will not be imprinted upon their soul's papyrus.

Our last sight of this day's full sun is finally sinking beneath the horizon, and this evening's ceremony begins, called to life by the pure devotion of hearts aflame with songs of love for all.

THE OM OF THE COSMOS

"He who was born of old was born of water. Right from the
Waters, the Soul drew forth and shaped a person."
—from the *Upanishads*

The Ganga flows through all time. It journeys white-capped down rocky crevices and sweeps through thick green, sweet-scented forests of the Himalayas, past tenuous patchwork homes of mudbrick and scrap wood, and past weather-bleached temples and towns. It falls from these gigantic mountains onto the plains and continues traveling a path of earth and rock worn clean over the multiple millenniums of its unending existence on its alternately swift and sluggish course to the ocean.

A map traces the Ganga's course through India and the region of Bengal till it flows out to the sea from its multiple tributaries that spill into the Bay of Bengal. Yet, I've come to know it runs through the veins and capillaries of the lives of all of us everywhere. Its current carries us forward from each past life to the next and on into our future, even as it washes us free of any trouble, doubt, or pain we offer to it. In the rhythm and melody of its enduring, strong tide is the secret of life. Listen to its song and you feel the OM of the cosmos reverberate inside the cells of your being. It's a brackish and awesome blue, brown, green, silver, clear delight to see from wherever you are.

Stand upon its banks at the holy city of Rishikesh and see and think and hear nothing but its current sweeping beyond you. Unflex the muscles of your thoughts and leave everything you know behind. Drink energy, rest, memory, wisdom, and inspiration from this sacred moving pool of faith.

As when wrapped in the embracing, warm, comforting arms of a loving mother, the caress of this river allows you to rest. Let it carry the strains and disappointments of your life and unfulfilled dreams downstream for awhile. Unburdened, life now feels lighter, a little easier. The journey has been long. Most of us don't even remember what it was we started out in search of. So, just sitting, resting unencumbered, feels really good. You stretch and breathe more freely with an emptied backpack. You may wonder why and how you carried this weight for so long—or perhaps such thoughts may only come later. . . .

You can taste the Ganga. It dances bedazzled on currents of air and lays upon the epidermis of your flesh. Its quickness, its coolness refreshes, and its energy begins seeping beneath the material layers of your structured existence, drowning and revitalizing the honeycomb fabric of your life. Feel a tingle?

"What is it about this place?" you wonder. "What am I feeling? What is happening?"

The Ganga, its brilliance and its swirling crusty depth, entices. You can't resist. You stare, trying to snorkel your awareness beneath its surface and listen to the sounds that whisper and chorus and call to you. Something . . . something vague begins tickling your brain. What is this? What memory is awakening? Is there something you've forgotten? What is it you feel—must remember?

The river flows unceasingly, taking what is given and giving what is needed. Sit and be with it. Let yourself flow with it. Watch it. You'll notice that it never disappears from sight. It will merely round a bend and go beyond that which you, as yet, can see. Without worry, without strategy, the aorta of the Ganga flows, serving and feeding the spiritual and physical kingdoms of the land, animals, plants, and humanity that find their way to it.

Watch those people who come to its banks; watch those who come in the blackness preceding every morning's dawn and in the fading light preceding the setting of the evening. Singly, old and young, strong and weak, they walk. Some shuffle. Others crawl. Their thin or even ragged clothing is no barrier to the wind or weather, yet the people bring their bodies, their faith, and a brass or tin cup to the river. Mother Ganga draws them like the magnetic north draws a compass needle to the source of its directional bearing.

Life recycles and is re-fortified in the churn and swirl and swoosh of the Ganga. The people's quiet, simple devotion and faith are fed by this river. Station does not matter; nationality, sex, color does not matter. The river accepts all castes and honors all beliefs. To the water, all are one. When will we know as much as water?

Consider the busy-ness of our lives; how hard it is to get out of bed when all we have to look forward to are the beautiful warm surroundings of our homes and possessions and a fresh-brewed cup of coffee before starting our well-paid work day. Yet, I sense there are greater considerations known by and offered in the prayer-raised arms of these strangers. Daily I watch them walking a far-from-convenient-path to this river to make a chaste two-minute offering to Something they sense to be greater than themselves and which most of us are too busy to even think about: God—Life.

There are men of business along this strip of town commerce who open their stalls each morning without thinking about God. It is not hard to tell those of faith and those too busy or too calloused to pay homage. The seismic quaking of their too busy thoughts vibrates from their every word and deed—and is obvious in the aftershocks of their every interaction.

The dichotomy between such faiths, and between their lives and ours, humbles and inspires—if you allow it. It is easier not to consider such things. It is easier while traveling in India to snap photographs of listless, hungry cows chewing newspapers picked off cobblestone streets; easier to buy the trinkets displayed on glass shelves; more fun to write postcards telling family and friends nothing of substance and, perhaps, some judgment about what we see here.

How different life would be if we all allowed ourselves to hear the *whoosh* of this river, listen to some of the stories it carries about the eternity of life and the lives we've lived and can no longer easily recall, tell some of our tales to it, and accept Ma Ganga's offer to hold them for us for awhile and allow life to be as harmonious, easy, compassionate, abundant, and devoted as God desires the rivers of all our lives to be.

The river is instinctive, sure, and ever faithful. Those wisdoms that are carried for each of us to drink upon its waters spring from the source of its existence, which is the source of our own, and our essence continually seeks such wisdom in the journey of our many lives to realize ourselves at One with God—and all of life.

Go to the river . . . or . . . just listen to the steady swirl and churning of it rising within *you*. Hear the *OM* of the cosmos. Feel the sparkle of light that sings and dances within the spring of your own soul. Be One with the water and taste how refreshing every thought, word, and deed feels. Consider the many others who will feel refreshed as they stand upon the sands around you, feeling *your* bright waves swirl and sway upon the shores of their lives.

MOONLIGHT ON THE GANGA

"Let the waters settle
You will see stars and moon
mirrored in your Being."
—from *Rumi: Fragments, Ecstasies* interpretive compilation by
Daniel Liebert

The sound of *OM* is said to be the primordial sound of the cosmos—the creation and the life. In the flow and chortle and sweep of the River Ganga, Omnipotence rises from, resonates with, and washes every cell of who I am and am becoming because *OM*, creation, the life, and omnipotence is ingrained within every single being. This sound of the One churning atoms, droplets, waves, and its surging current releases the tabla of my own frequency in motion because finally, for whatever reason, I am, at long last, poised within and attuned to hear and BE.

It is a natural resonance we share, for humans and the earth are both physically composed primarily of water. Over 65% of the human body is water, and tidal oceans cover over 70% of the earth. Yet, besides this, it is also now known that we are not as solidly formed as once believed; that, in fact, between *every* one of the minutest of the sub-sub-subest molecular structures of *everything* (including water), there is—nothing. Space. Silence. Stillness. OM. The sound of silence that vibrates and roars with potential, with life, with . . . God. Stars may ceiling the blackness of a clear evening sky and seem sometimes to overlap, but still there is vast space between each. What happens when you rest in the silence of one of those deep spaces within yourself?

A tempest of unearthly wind has been unleashed upon Rishikesh this night, unfurling and flapping and agitating every living limb and branch and leaf like crazed flags amast roaming ships at sea. I'm awake, though barely, standing on the stairway feeling the thunder of every leafy impact against the convulsing blast. Something, *something* is up. That knowing fragrance lances my intuition like the thorn of a rose might flesh, and I step into the path of the whirling wind, the patter of my bare feet slapping and cracking on the cold concrete as upon ice coating a mountain lake.

Have you ever rested upon a sacred river and felt the moon rise and grow and glow inside you?

How ironic, I think, that I've been drawn from my bed so early in the predawn morning following a filament of invisible string that's reeled me, cold and unkempt, to the river's edge to find, not the subtle, tie-dyed ribbons of the rising sun, but a pregnant full moon poised high and wide upon the hillside's thighs, birthing its lifeblood, dancing and sparkling upon the trembling, surging stream.

A warm froth fills my chest, and I let myself fall upon her soft belly, fingers floating free upon her, while my mind wanders within her waves, and lunar dreams lace bright beads beneath the cloth of my skin. Every moment dissolves into this eternal one of watching and feeling this basking moon. Her girth, so ripe and round and full seems almost capable of sinking the earth should she choose to rest the whole of her weight upon us. Her luminary beams reveal that sometimes the conscious search is found unconsciously, sometimes it is not our will, but our willingness to follow Another's, that illuminates our path.

I notice there is light even in dark. I may have chosen to occupy my life with other things and ignore it before, but, nonetheless and forever, light shimmers and waits silently to be noticed; and when it is, light revels, quivering in the pleasured grasp of understanding.

A blush of eerie, vaporous silver glows to the surface of the speeding, neon-ebony river from its deep recesses while the jazillion fermenting lights falling from the rapturous moon squiggle to life upon her arching, racing waves. Overhead, stars have spilled like white sand across the oceanic heavens, the earth-bound river and infinite sky seeming to mirror the lights of each other.

I'm cellophaned betwixt and between these awesome vistas that feel like membranes of my own skin, their every particle prickling molecules of mine and stirring them awake. Inaudible conversations enrapture me, tingling and teasing each synapse wired within my skin.

Every moment should be like this, I think.

Every moment is . . . or can be. It's me who isn't. There are moments that call, that whisper, that cry, that laugh, that holler; moments that dance and moments that sing; there are moments of silence clanging loud as steeple bells, and moments throbbing deep as bass drums; moments I've let slip past, unaware behind my veil of unconscious sleep that life transfuses and is transformed in such a moment.

Nothing is ever the same after such a moment. Place pure diamonds upon the flesh of your neck and fakes will never quite sparkle, can never satisfy again. Dazzling diamonds falling from moonbeams tantalize the waters of the coursing stream I'm watching. They wash over the internal dam I've constructed to protect me. Ignited by their light, I sense no need to protect, to defend, to attack, and no need to stumble in the dark again.

What really is life supposed to be? In moments at once so sublime and invigorating as this, it's easy to forget my toil, how hard it is to make life happen the way I want it to, the rules defining "how things are and how you will do and think about things." Now, however, some soul-full conversation urges me that such rules are to be discarded and life replenished, re-landscaped in the light of a new vision. When our eyesight improves, we chuck our old glasses, right?

Things can never be the same again. The trembling light of this night reflects something of the person I really am, or am to become; and the waking of my own luminous moon, sand-drenched sky, star-bright water, and agitating wind will glow and gale forever more— not as a bitter storm or insomniac worries, or pensive hopes and idle wishes—but a sure vision of what life will be, what we will all make it.

Before this morning, I've accepted life the same as most other people have accepted it to be, or at least how I've assumed most others have. I've accepted it in the form of the words and deeds "done" and "taught" to me, broadcast media images, the rules and leaders assigned to me, and I've reflected my vision of life in every thought, word, and deed I've dealt towards others. Some of these now sting! Yet, I don't know *anyone* who likes the way things are, and even the habitual complaints we make sound like the rhythmic *clickity-clack, clickity-clack* of trains riding tracks on prescribed routes and lulling their passengers to sleep.

Divinity's opiate, however, inspires to wakefulness.

I'm tasting the sacred river's enticing thoughts teaspoonful by teaspoonful and allowing them to bubble and birth new knowings in me. Meanwhile, the fragrance of the sacred river rises upon dangling moonbeams, rinsing and re-oxygenating every corpuscle and fiber of the body I have, and the sparks from its infinite song rekindle my flagging spirit that yearns so much for peace, for love, for the acceptance of happiness in my life, which yearns for a fine grace.

Yes, in the silence between and *within* everything, there is . . . Space . . . Stillness . . . Om . . . Potential . . . God. There is remembrance, the *thrill* of sensing something to remember. And, in the silence between people and *within* every person, there is Space . . . Stillness . . . Om . . . Potential . . . God, because there can be *nothing* really separating anything when it is filled with so much.

When you rest in the silence of one of those deep spaces, you're filled with the real "stuff" of life, and nothing can ever be the same again, because illusions of separation, and distinction of difference, of higher and lower, of better or worse, all the definitions of who you are and I am and how things will be are transformed in the blink of an eye. . . . This final trump sounds for everyone in their own time.

The spectral sights and enduring sounds of the celestial chorus *OM* rise over the octave waves during the many moments I am sitting here. Soon I'll witness the cyclical rise of the golden sun's glory. Soon we all will—metaphorically. It's riding the current of our memories and desires for something . . . something better, and the current of that thought has started everybody suspecting "something's up." By stepping outside and leaving momentary comforts behind to follow an instinct for something that called to me on the wind, I've heard unspoken mysteries whispered in the light of darkness heralding new life, peace.

It is something which cannot NOT be, because it already breathes in the silent stillness of everything that already is. Its promise is the heartbeat of the earth. Its pulse throbs within our chests. Moved by its current, feeling it stretched like fine silk within all of the all, accepting it as the very fabric of the "I" that I am illuminates every potential for peace in my life's moment by moment birthing of thoughts, words, and deeds. These feed, sustain, inspire me, and inspire other people, as theirs will inspire me.

I always want to feel the skin of this luscious lunar orb on my own, the light of dancing stars, the warmth of a cold, turbulent breeze, be dazzled by water thick with arcing waves, smell the scent of jasmine in winter, and watch rainbow ribbons ripple from the gilded sun. It's an intoxication that cures, because even more than these divine, sensory delights, I want to know everyone is fed, and I want to care and love in abundance so that everyone may sense their own peace.

A call to arms rises from my very soul, erupting unbidden, un-suspected, surfacing through epidermal and ethereal layers, shouting with its so long held breath—"Bring peace to earth."

The desire houses sparks of prophetic fulfillment. In the sparks dance the answers that can be glimpsed but not realized in any guide-book. In living the answers, we realize it all. This, I think, is what it's really all about.

I have sung songs at sunrise upon the rooftop of this ashram with the others whom I've traveled here with, and now one verse means so much to me: "Let there be peace on earth and let it begin with me."

The song itself has never before been a favorite of mine. I suspect that says a lot about the kind of person I've been and the other types of priorities I've had. Yet, its essence is now the blood feeding each piece of me, and I'm flushed with its power. It seems, indeed, the be-lief's been shimmering aura-like within and around every experience, conversation, sight, scent, emotion, and thought I've availed myself of while here.

It's a powerful belief—peace—that's spoken of and prepared for by holy ones throughout all time—Krishna, Buddha, Zarathustra, Mohammed, Jesus, ad infinitum. Peace on earth, heaven on earth. The same message has flowed to earth in water through the locks of a god's hair, in the subtle power of parables spoken by holy ones, on the rays of each day's rising sun and the suffused glow of evening's moon, and it is kept vital in the beating of our hearts and in the birthing springs of life's renewal.

This is the breathless beauty of a life too long denied. It tastes ripe, sweet, succulent, satisfying. It is the river that flows through each one of us, and when it fills us and spills beyond our personal embankments, it floods the surrounding fields with nutrients and washes distressed soil. Imagine being the peace that helps others feel their own. Imagine being the peace that recreates itself. Imagine being the peace God has created us to be.

Ride the current of the river and reflect it from within you. . . . Everything will change. . . .

"There are no maps; no more creeds or philosophies. From here on in, the directions come straight from the Universe."
—Akshara Noor

Thank you for what has been written before . . .

Each chapter of *Moonlight on the Ganga* opens with what might be described as 'thematic quotes' specific to some aspect of that chapter's experiences. Readers, know that you have also benefited in some way from those written words offered by others.

The Ganges: A Personal Encounter, by Edward Rice. Copyright 1974 by Edward Rice. Reprinted with permission of Simon and Schuster Books for Young Readers, an imprint of Simon and Schuster Children's Publishing Division.

Mother Ganges, by Sri Swami Sivananda, courtesy of The Divine Life Society.

The Essene Gospel of Peace, Book One and *The Essene Gospel of Peace, Book Two*, translated by Edmond Bordeaux Szekeley; courtesy of Mrs. (Norma) Edmond Bordeaux Szekeley and The International Biogenic Society, P.O. Box 849, Nelson, British Columbia, Canada V1L 6A5.

St. John of the Cross: The Poems; quotes from "Songs Between the Soul and the Bridegroom," as translated by Roy Campbell. Copyright 1951; Permission courtesy of his daughter, Teresa Campbell. This work is newly released by Harvill Press, London, in 2000.

Enchantment of the World: India, by Sylvia McNair. Copyright 1990. Published by Children's Press. Courtesy of Grolier Publishing.

Mutant Message Down Under, by Marlo Morgan. Copyright 1994. Published by and permission received from HarperCollins.

On God and Man, by Ralph Waldo Emerson. Published in 1961. Courtesy of Peter Pauper Press.

Slowly Down the Ganges, by Eric Newby. Copyright 1966. Recently republished in the U.S. by Lonely Planet Publications. Permission courtesy of Lonely Planet and HarperCollins Publishers Ltd., London.

Jawaharlal Nehru, first Prime Minister of India after the country's independence, who in public speeches and even in his Last Will and Testament, expressed his homage and love of the Ganga.

Rumi: Fragments, Ecstasies, interpretive compilations by Daniel Liebert. Published by and permission received from Omega Publications, 256 Darrow Road, New Lebanon, N.Y.

Finally, we all owe tremendous gratitude to the original writers of the many holy texts that have come down to us through the ages—whether it be the *Mahabharata,* including the more popularly known *Bhagavad Gita,* as well as the *Uphanishads, The Bible,* and others. Their messages continually exhort us to remember the nobility of being human as we live and create as the light of God.

And I personally look forward to the day, not far off from these years, when new scrolls and discoveries will unveil greater truths in the awareness of us all. May what has not been exactly accurate in what we have been taught be blessed and easily released, so that what has come down to us in written form through the ages of and from Spirit that *is* true can be newly rejoined with the finest of what has been for so long hidden from our sights, for the benefit of all.

ACKNOWLEDGMENTS

"I shall return to you."

Each of us, I believe, have had such a pledge spoken to us during our heavenly lives-between-lifetimes by some soul who is meant to draw us back to remembrance of our essence. And, in some ways, each of us have made similar pledges.

As an adult, I'd forgotten my childhood pledges to myself that "I won't settle," as I'd observed adults did. Instead, I'd entered the business world and accepted promotions and raises, traveled, filled my free time with fun, and deluded myself into believing I was independent and free.

Not until I stepped off that path, unsure but open to whatever might occur, did a new, completely different vision of how life was meant to be lived and who I might truly be come into focus.

Reader . . . this book, and the person I am and who I am continuing to become, owes eternal gratitude to Jacqueline T. Snyder, spiritual visionary, author, and proud mother of two sons, whose values, beliefs, complete faith and trust in God, and whose profound teachings first opened me to the more of who I might truly be. It was she who organized this trip to India. Her memory is alive still in mine, and I acknowledge the potency of her divine teachings herein.

Most especially, for allowing me to look into the eyes of eternity and feel and experience the awesome essence of divine love and guidance, I offer my gratitude and love to Z. Upon these pages I live and renew my promise.

To my mother, Adele, and father, Chester, whose love, strengths, values, and happiness allowed me to always feel safe, and offered me the freedom to express and grow—I love you.

Also, I acknowledge the presence and support of Denise Butler who has experienced and enjoyed more than she'd ever suspected possible during all the years we've known each other.

Incredible gratitude is owed and acknowledged to author Suzane Piela who *urged* me not to put this manuscript back in the closet when yet another rejection letter was received.

To my Daybue editor, Elizabeth Day, whose touching and inspirational rejection letter, received on the heel of so many others, offered me insight into how this book might truly touch others. . . . And so, enlivened by her praise and prodded by Suzane, I trusted, lit a candle, and asked God for assistance in realigning the work and editing anything that interfered with and did not serve its highest purpose. I thank Elizabeth for accepting the revised version of that first edition.

As well, I'm grateful to the lives of joy embodied in my faithful dogs, Dash, Fable, and Storm, who—usually—forgave me when this manuscript took me from them.

There are others who have offered me the strength and enjoyment of their friendship, presence, and support. Big hugs to Sheila Kenny, artist Dolly Meymand, artist Sharon Walker, Linda Joy, Sabrina Fox, Lenedra Carroll, and all my other "Sacred Life" family. Each holds a place for Spirit to live, and breath, and have its being—as do you.

AUTHOR BIOGRAPHY

Author and freelance writer Claire Krulikowski left a 20-year business and management career in the mid 1990's to return to her love of writing and ponder her life's purpose. A meeting with an American woman mystic years later and a trip to India birthed the writing of *Moonlight on the Ganga*, the first of her three previously published books. Check her website: www.clairekrulikowski.com

CPSIA information can be obtained
at www.ICGtesting.com
Printed in the USA
BVOW08s1604060517
483183BV00001B/2/P